Reading Instruction in the Middle School
(A Whole School Approach)

**By Maryann Murphy Manning
and Gary L. Manning**

National Education Association
Washington, D.C.

Copyright © 1979
National Education Association of the United States

Stock No. 1707-2-00 (paper)

Library of Congress Cataloging in Publication Data

Manning, Maryann Murphy.
    Reading instruction in the middle school.

    Bibliography:
      1. Reading (Secondary education)   2. Middle schools.
I. Manning, Gary L., joint author. II. Title.
LB1632.M27   428'.4'0712   79-4427
ISBN 0-8106-1707-2

Reading Instruction
in the Middle School
(A Whole School Approach)

CONTENTS

The Authors

Drs. Gary and Maryann Manning are Associate Professors of Education at the University of Alabama, Birmingham.

The Consultants

The following educators have reviewed the manuscript and provided helpful comments and suggestions: Vivian Arthur, Language Arts Teacher, Grand County Middle School, Moab, Utah; Dr. Arthur E. Garner, Associate Professor of Education, Memphis State University, Tennessee; Eunice E. Gyger, seventh grade Remedial Reading teacher, North Junior High School, Omaha, Nebraska; Jan Kuker, Reading teacher, James Bowie Jr. High School, Amarillo, Texas; Janis Sparkman, classroom teacher, Decatur Middle School, Decatur, Alabama.

INTRODUCTION

This book has two major purposes: to present a rationale for a developmental reading program in the middle school and to provide middle school teachers with concrete suggestions for teaching reading.

Middle school teachers are concerned that students in middle schools improve their reading skills. We agree that reading instruction is one of the important missions of the middle school. It is the responsibility of all schools to teach reading, and of middle school teachers to improve the reading abilities and foster the reading interests of their students. But how does one teach reading in the middle school? There is certainly no single solution to this problem. We will discuss here several ideas or alternatives for the middle school teacher.

Teachers hear a great deal about individualization these days, but educators define individualization in different ways. For some it means that all students are working on different skills and different activities. This concept of individualization frightens many teachers who doubt they can manage a group of students each working on different skills.

We believe that individualization means developing individual students to their optimum levels. There are many ways teachers can work toward this goal — in small group, large group, and one-to-one settings. These approaches will be discussed, and materials and activities to help teachers in their attempts to meet students' needs will be described.

We will also describe readers who exhibit different reading needs. We do not mean to imply that there are only three types of readers, or that readers should be grouped and separated on the basis of ability. Rather we hope to illustrate the many reading profiles of middle school students and suggest that options exist for teachers who are striving to provide appropriate reading instruction for these students.

Experienced teachers recognize there are many barriers to implementing a quality individualized reading program. Departmentalization, where the instructor teaches several different groups of students each day, is one major barrier. Others include short periods, large classes, and few materials. If teachers are to eliminate or minimize these barriers, they should become involved in curriculum decision-making processes.

This book is organized into five major sections. In the first two chapters we present an overview of middle school philosophy and the rationale for including reading instruction in the middle school program. Section Two (Chapters 3 and 4) provides practical suggestions for teachers who wish to develop appropriate reading activities for students at different ability levels. In Section Three (Chapters 5 and 6) we examine the various content areas of the middle school curriculum and suggest how teachers of these content areas can stress reading improvement. Section Four (Chapter 7) suggests ways to increase recreational reading among students. Finally in Section Five (Chapter 8) we discuss ways to evaluate reading programs in the middle school.

Throughout this book, we find ourselves faced with a choice between what is ideal and what is practical. Much being written or said today is at the ideal level. Ideally, middle school students will receive reading instruction in an individual or small group setting, assisted by trained personnel with unlimited resources of time and energy. Ideally, students are given appropriate reading materials in all content areas with directed reading activities designed to help them improve their reading skills in each area.

Realistically, teachers are often confronted with too many students, too few materials, and not enough time in which to implement an ideal program. The practical approach calls for teachers to take a look at the options available to them within the limitations of their particular situations. We hope this book provides some practical suggestions for caring teachers in middle schools and that these suggestions offer challenges and the promise of rewards.

CHAPTER 1
READING — A VITAL PART
OF THE MIDDLE SCHOOL
CURRICULUM

Reading instruction for the ten- to fourteen-year-old has traditionally received little attention. The assumption was that teaching reading was the job of elementary school teachers and that little could be done for students who reached the middle-school level lacking the necessary reading skills. If poor readers received any attention, it was provided by English teachers who often had little or no specialized training in reading instruction.

More and more, teachers of middle school students are learning to provide quality reading programs. Instructors realize they can help students who have reading problems as well as those who are already good readers. An increasing number of content area teachers are helping students improve reading skills as reading becomes an integral part of the middle school program.

NATURE OF MIDDLE SCHOOLS

The middle school movement, much like the junior high school movement earlier in this century, is committed to creating a unique curriculum for the ten- to fourteen-year-old. Teachers of these youngsters are challenged to develop and implement learning environments tailored to the needs and abilities of this age group.

Middle school pupils are a challenge to teachers because of their diversity in physical, social, emotional, and intellectual characteristics. When Piaget's stages of intellectual development are considered, we realize that middle school children range from those who understand only the real and concrete to those who are able to think theoretically and abstractly. Middle school pupils of today are different from those of a generation ago. They are maturing faster physically, probably due to improved nutrition, disease prevention, and better medical care. In addition, these youngsters have a different perspective of the world, possibly because they are more aware of the "shrinking world" through increased exposure to media.

Strickland and Alexander[22] suggest the educational program for students between the ages of ten and fourteen serves several purposes:

1. To serve the educational needs of the "in-between-agers" (older children, preadolescents, early adolescents) in a school coming between the school for earlier childhood and the high school

2. To provide optimum individualization of curriculum and instruction for a population characterized by great variability

3. In relation to the foregoing aims, to plan, implement, evaluate, and modify, in a continuing curriculum development program, a curriculum that provides for (a) a planned sequence of concepts in the general education areas, (b) major emphasis on the interests and skills for continued learning, (c) a balanced program of exploratory experiences and other activities and services for personal development, and (d) appropriate attention to the development of values

4. To promote continuous progress through and smooth articulation between the several phases and levels of the total educational program

5. To facilitate the optimum use of personnel and facilities available for continuing improvement of schooling.

Several of these points have direct implications for reading instruction. Purpose Two states that middle school students are greatly different from one another and the educational program must be individualized in order to meet those differences. Middle school teachers recognize there is a wide range of reading ability among their students. Teachers should therefore try to identify the differences and make accommodations for those differences.

As related to reading, Purpose Three suggests that the reading program needs to be developed and modified on a continuing basis. Teachers need to identify the reading interests and skill development levels of their students so they can plan an appropriate reading program.

Purpose Four implies that middle school teachers need to take up where elementary school teachers leave off. The successful elementary teacher emphasizes the decoding and comprehending processes of reading and uses appropriate methods and materials to teach these processes. Middle school teachers need to employ many of the same instructional strategies to overcome the reading deficiencies of many of their students.

A WHOLE SCHOOL APPROACH

How can we describe a middle school reading program? Fillmer[9] makes the following recommendations appropriate for middle school reading instruction:

1. A discrete reading program should exist in the middle school both to improve reading skills and to help pupils learn to receive personal satisfaction from reading.
2. This program should be individualized to meet the needs of adolescents as they perceive those needs.
3. Students should keep personal records of progress in reading and have regular opportunities to confer with the reading teacher.
4. The reading program should help pupils satisfy the need for intellectual development by helping them develop reading-related skills for continued learning.
5. The reading program should help readers to experience vicariously attitudes, concerns, feelings, and values that they may not be able to experience directly.
6. The reading program should provide students with an informational base for creative oral and dramatic interaction with their classmates on value clarification activities.
7. The reading program should make available to pupils a variety of reading materials on a wide range of topics and levels of readability.

Middle school educators are interested in implementing such a reading program. But to ensure a successful program, the whole school, faculty and administration, must become committed to and involved in the reading concept. Several steps can be taken to guarantee whole-school support. The first step is the establishment of a reading committee.

ESSENTIALS FOR A READING COMMITTEE

Middle schools should have a reading committee made up of guidance counselors, librarians, content area teachers, reading teachers, administrators, and other specialized personnel. Burmeister[4] suggests the duties of this committee include:

1. Determining a philosophy of reading
2. Determining ways of diagnosing students' needs in reading skills
3. Deciding what kinds of materials teachers should be encouraged to purchase
4. Recommending schoolwide grouping plans
5. Helping teachers group students and individualize instruction in the classroom
6. Showing teachers how to recognize the need for specific types of skill development and showing them how to satisfy these needs
7. Showing teachers the value of the Directed Reading Activity, SQ3R, building interests, etc.
8. Determining how the schoolwide reading program can be coordinated and providing such coordination
9. Determining methodology and materials to be used in evaluating the successes and failures of the program
10. Determining policies to be used in inservice training.

READING TEACHERS

Middle schools that have trained reading specialists are fortunate. These reading teachers can communicate to the entire faculty the special needs of students in the remedial program. These specialists can also provide useful suggestions and support to content area teachers in the area of reading.

LANGUAGE ARTS TEACHERS

Students differ greatly in the skills of writing, handwriting, spelling, listening, speaking, and reading. As much as possible, language arts teachers should individualize instruction to meet the needs of each student. If teachers are to accomplish this important task, they must be given adequate time to work with students and must have a variety of materials at their disposal.

CONTENT AREA TEACHERS

Content areas can be an arena for reading improvement if teachers can provide for reading differences through use of such strategies as multilevel texts and nonprint media. Cooperative planning and sharing of materials can reinforce and encourage effective instruction.

ADMINISTRATORS

Teachers need administration leadership and support if an effective whole-school reading program is to be implemented. Administrators can show their support by participating on the reading committee and supporting other teacher efforts. There must be budgetary commitments to staff development, reading materials, and reading teachers. Administrators must work with teachers to develop effective scheduling that will facilitate implementation of the reading programs.

GUIDANCE COUNSELORS

Guidance counselors can help teachers gather data useful in determining needs of students, in evaluating the school's reading program, and in establishing future directions for that program.

MEDIA SPECIALISTS

Media specialists can significantly increase teacher effectiveness by providing teachers and students with materials at all levels of reading difficulty and materials that appeal to various interests for use in remedial and developmental reading. Content area teachers can obtain from the media specialist topic materials written for readers at various skill levels and a variety of nonprint materials.

THE CHALLENGE

When the staff members in a middle school make concerted efforts to improve reading instruction, improvement will always occur. Cooperative effort ensures the best results. Improved reading is not the responsibility of the language arts and reading teachers alone; it is a responsibility shared by the entire professional staff. Good reading programs don't just happen, they are planned.

CHAPTER 2
AS DIFFERENT AS DAY AND NIGHT —
THE VARIED READERS

Middle school students differ from one another in terms of social, emotional, physical, and intellectual development. As they undergo rapid physical changes, they must simultaneously make many psychological and social adjustments. Rapid mental growth accompanies these changes and adjustments.

Students in the ten to fourteen age group also differ widely in achievement. Goodlad[12] in *School, Curriculum, and the Individual* writes:

> The broad spread from high to low achiever steadily increases with an upward movement of heterogenous classes (relatively homogenous in chronological age) through the school. In the intermediate grades, this spread is approximately the number of years designated by the number of grade-level: that is, by the third grade, three years; by the fourth grade, four years; by the fifth grade, five years. However, since the spread in achievement accelerates slightly faster than a year-per-year of schooling, the overall range in junior high school classes is approximately two-thirds the median chronological age of the groups.
>
> In subject areas, such as reading and language arts, where children can readily proceed on their own in a variety of out-of-school situations, the spread from high to low achiever frequently is one and one-half to twice the number of the grade level. Hence, in the fifth grade, there frequently is an eight year spread in reading achievement between the best and poorest readers.

Middle school students fall into three broad groups: (1) accelerated readers who read "above grade level" materials with no difficulty, (2) "on grade level" readers who, with guidance, can read printed materials written for their grade level, and (3) remedial readers who, even with guidance, have great difficulty with materials written for their grade level. Within these groups, we can also expect a wide range of differences, all of which have implications for instructional planning.

ASSESSMENT

Given this high degree of variability, how do teachers plan successful reading programs? A first step is to determine the general reading levels of the students. This information may already be available from scores on reading subtests and from written observations made by teachers.

Students' grades in content areas might give a clue as to reading ability. Many times, however, assigned grades are not accurate indicators of reading level. Students who receive high grades may indeed be excellent readers or they may be average readers who possess very good study habits. Similarly, not all students who receive low grades have reading difficulties; when excellent readers are not motivated, they sometimes receive poor grades.

Each student's reading achievement should be measured as that student enters the middle school. Teacher evaluations are critical here. Teachers from the feeder elementary schools should be asked to complete a simple form for each student to assist the middle school teacher with assessment.

Testing is another evaluation tool. If an achievement test with a reading subtest has not been administered within the last year, a reading test should be given. Standardized tests, criterion-referenced tests, informal inventories, or a combination of these tests can be adminstered to obtain more complete information. Teachers also need data that reflect students' abilities in decoding words, comprehension, vocabulary, and study skills.

Test scores should be viewed with caution, however. Reading achievement scores should be used only as a rough guide in determining students' instructional needs. Ideally, teachers should administer both informal reading inventories and diagnostic tests to get a detailed picture of students' strengths and needs. Certainly if students have severe reading problems, it is necessary that both kinds of tests be administered. However, since administering the two types of tests is a time-consuming process, it may not be necessary for all students. Again, it is important to remember that teacher observation provides the best verification that test data are accurate.

MIDDLE SCHOOL STUDENTS AS READERS

There are three different kinds of readers in the middle schools: the accelerated reader, the "on grade level" reader, and the remedial reader. Once general reading level has been assessed, more specific information can be gathered on each student.

THE ACCELERATED READERS: ALL SYSTEMS GO

These readers have little or no difficulty with decoding words or comprehension, though some have problems with rate or study skills, and some need to improve and increase their vocabulary. Examples of the accelerated reader are Mary Sue the Bookworm, and James the Capable Reader Who Doesn't.

Mary Sue is the typical studious pupil, and printed symbols have always been "duck soup" for her. At one year she turned the pages of the book her mother read to her at bedtime, and she easily recognized the names of her favorite cereals by the age of two and a half. At four years, she was printing her name and was beginning to read the Dr. Seuss easy readers. Teachers didn't know how to challenge her in kindergarten and in first grade because she was so far ahead of the class. Motivating Mary Sue to read is no problem. She has books in her own personal bedroom library and devours anything given to her at school. She is seldom without a book, usually a book for older readers.

James is a capable reader, but he doesn't read. He crawled at an early age and walked at nine months. Though he liked to listen to his mother and father read, he was more interested in moving around. In kindergarten and first grade he mastered everything that was presented, but reading was not his idea of recreation. Little League baseball and Peewee football are his idea of the way to spend free time. On achievement tests he scores several notches above grade level, but his teachers are concerned that he doesn't like to read and doesn't read at a very efficient rate.

Teachers in the middle school are often confronted with

students like Mary Sue and James, students who need only a minimal amount of help. In order to provide for them, the teacher may use an evaluation sheet similar to the one below:

Accelerated Readers (X indicates that help is needed)

Student's Name	Compre-hension	Pronun-ciation	Rate	Vocab-ulary	Study Skills	Interest
Mary Sue			X			
James			X		X	X

A chart like this one helps content area teachers provide for students who need little if any help with reading. In Chapter 4 there are specific suggestions for teaching these students.

THE "ON GRADE LEVEL" READERS: SAILING ALONG

These readers are usually able to handle most materials written at their grade level. (Teachers should remember, however, that not all textbooks are written at the grade level for which they are used. Readability checks reveal that some textbooks are at an ability level as much as two or more grades above the designated grade.) This group needs what have often been referred to as developmental reading activities. Reading instruction needs to be a part of their language arts curriculum, and content area teachers in particular need to use strategies, such as a directed reading activity, whenever they assign printed materials. This approach is explained in detail in Chapters 5 and 6.

Susan the Conscientious Student and Daniel the Charmer represent two students who read at grade level. Daniel has always been known for his good personality. At six months, he won the smile award in a baby beauty contest. When a sociogram is administered, he is always a leader, and teachers, other adults, and classmates like him. He isn't such a star in academics, however. He doesn't receive bad grades, but neither does he excel. He finishes assignments on time and usually receives an average grade. While he doesn't like to read entire books, he does read sport magazines and short mystery stories. Daniel doesn't have trouble recognizing words in textbooks, but he doesn't always comprehend as well as one would expect. He is the closest thing to an average student one could expect to find.

Susan has always been a favorite of her teachers. Helpful and not demanding a lot of attention, she always receives a superior grade in conduct. Her teachers would not call her a super student, but neither would they classify her as slow. She comprehends best when she reads for a specific purpose. If Susan doesn't understand, she asks for help. She has been in the average reading group since first grade and seems interested in school. Susan doesn't cause worries for her teachers.

The content area teacher and the language arts teacher may wish to use a chart like the one below to summarize the needs of average students like Daniel and Susan:

On Grade Level Readers (X indicates that help is needed)

Student's Name	Decoding	Compre-hension	Pronun-ciation	Rate	Vocab-ulary	Study Skills	Interest
Daniel		X		X	X		X
Susan				X		X	

While these students do not need to devote large amounts of time to intensive reading instruction, some guidance is necessary. Too often reading is not taught in the middle grades, but reading instruction is very important for students like Daniel and Susan. Specific suggestions for working with these readers are given in Chapter 4.

THE "BELOW GRADE LEVEL" READERS: HELP! HELP!

Remedial readers are unable to read grade level materials. They offer a serious challenge to middle school teachers committed to developing the reading potential of every student.

It is difficult to provide a general profile of the remedial reader. This group ranges in ability from the virtual nonreader to the reader who just needs a little push.

The *nonreader* has virtually no decoding skills. This student's history of failure to read has led to the development of negative attitudes, and the student may even brag, "I can't read." Often these students have self-concept and peer acceptance problems.

Jerry the Challenge is a typical nonreader. Childhood was not easy for Jerry. He was late to crawl and walk, and his language development was slow. There were few reading materials in Jerry's home, and since his parents didn't read very much for recreation or information, Jerry probably didn't perceive reading as important or fun. In first grade, Jerry just wasn't able to sit very long and listen to teachers or other students read. Seat work, such as practicing letters of the alphabet and coloring circles, didn't hold Jerry's interest. He was always in a low reading group, but his reading was even lower than that of others in the group. At this point in time, Jerry really doesn't think he can learn to read and, therefore, he seems to have lost the desire to read. He can, however, decode a few words, and with the direction of a teacher he can read very simple stories written at a primary level.

Teachers who work with students like Jerry need to use specific, carefully chosen reading methods. More important, they must be interested in these students and able to communicate that interest. Middle school teachers who are successful with these nonreaders may lack formal training in reading but communicate an "I know you can succeed" attitude to the student. The fewer students the teacher works with at one time and the longer the time available for reading instruction, the more successful will be the effort.

The *low level readers* can read only the simplest materials — low vocabulary, high interest materials. They can handle very little in the way of content area materials. These students usually have negative attitudes toward reading because of their record of failure. Teachers can make progress with these students by providing special instruction in reading skills tailored to each pupil's individual reading problem. A caring teacher can often prevent these students from becoming school dropouts.

Andrew the Passive Child is a low level reader. Andrew's pediatrician described him as a quiet baby who liked to sleep. He eventually mastered everything that other children did, but most development was months behind the average. His first attempts at learning to read were disastrous. Even the simplest readiness activities were difficult for Andrew. To make it even worse, Andrew has a sister two years younger who was reading simple books by age six. Consequently, he hates reading or any activity associated with reading. In middle school, Andrew can read at about the third grade level. So he is not a nonreader, but just a slow reader with a very negative attitude toward reading. His negative feelings are reinforced by failing grades and teacher and family displeasure. Even his peer group treats him as if he is dumb because he is not up to par in reading.

Another type of remedial reader needs *just a little push* to become an on grade level reader. These students can read textbooks but are often frustrated because they need help decoding and comprehending. These readers need a shot of motivation and extensive practice in reading. They require special attention but may not necessarily need specialized remedial teaching in reading.

An example of this sort of reader is Lottie the Underachiever. Lottie didn't walk or talk early, but neither was she extremely late. She enjoyed listening to books and would ask her kindergarten teacher to reread stories that she liked. She has a collection of books given to her by friends and grandparents. Kindergarten and first grade were smooth for Lottie, and in both years she scored above average on achievement tests. Everything was fine until Christmas of the second grade when Lottie developed pneumonia after a long illness with colds and flu. After a hospital stay of several weeks, she missed three months of school. Lottie's mother tried to help her with homework during this time, but even so she had begun to trail her classmates. Though she cannot read her textbooks, she manages to answer questions by listening in class. She doesn't hate to read, but she doesn't read very well. Now in seventh grade, Lottie is reading at least three years behind grade level.

Recordkeeping is important to help teachers summarize needs and establish programs for all these types of remedial readers. The following is an example of a general recordkeeping form:

Remedial Readers (X indicates that help is needed)

Student's Name	Decoding	Comprehension	Pronunciation	Rate	Vocabulary	Study Skills	Interest
Jerry	X	X	X	X	X	X	X
Andrew		X	X	X	X	X	X
Lottie				X	X	X	

PROVISIONS FOR IMPLEMENTING
A READING PROGRAM

Middle school teachers have discovered several methods for meeting the special reading needs of their students, and the following five organizational designs are considered especially appropriate: (1) a reading skills laboratory, (2) reading classes designed for special needs (not necessarily remedial), (3) individualized language arts programs, (4) reading instruction in the content areas, and (5) recreational reading. No one approach is complete in itself; a whole school reading program needs to incorporate all five designs.

A READING LABORATORY

A reading laboratory is an area within the middle school specifically designed to serve many remedial students, a place for developmental reading and study skill instruction. The reading laboratory staff could include reading teachers, aides, volunteers, peer tutors, and students from teacher training institutions.

In the laboratory students can find materials to assist them with improvement of reading skills. These resources might include low reading level, high-interest materials for remedial students, study skills materials, specific skills materials for students of all levels, and hardware designed to increase reading rate. Students may be scheduled into the lab for instruction or can be encouraged to go during independent learning periods.

SPECIAL READING CLASSES

Special reading classes for remedial students involves more than grouping a classroom of students on the basis of reading ability. These classes should be held apart from regular classroom activities, perhaps as a substitute for a given language arts period, during an independent study period, or in place of or in addition to other scheduled classes.

Remedial reading classes should be kept small if students are to realize improvements. During a fifty- to sixty-minute period, reading teachers can work with no more than a group of twelve to fifteen students. Progress often hinges on the special relationship the reading teacher develops with each student, and these relationships take time to foster. In order to be effective, the teacher also needs enough time to plan appropriate activities for each student.

Multileveled reading materials appropriate for the middle school student must be available to the special reading teacher. It is vital that teaching materials be appropriate for this level. A skill that has been introduced in the primary grades and must be retaught in the middle grades cannot be introduced with primary teaching materials, because materials intended for young children will turn off a middle schooler.

Special reading classes with trained teachers, adequate time, small class size, and appropriate materials can make the difference between success and disappointment in the reading skill development of middle school students.

INDIVIDUALIZED LANGUAGE ARTS PROGRAMS

Ideally, all language arts classes for middle school students are individualzied. With individualization, the reading needs of students at all grade levels can be accommodated: developmental reading materials are available at all reading levels and unmastered skills are developed individually or in small skill groups instituted for a short period of time.

This ideal is hardly ever achieved, however. For a variety of reasons, including large class size and departmentalization, it is often difficult to implement a totally individualized program. Even when such language arts classes are established, it is sometimes difficult for the teacher to give the low level reading students the time they need. For this reason, special reading classes and/or reading labs can complement an individualized language arts program.

READING IN THE CONTENT AREAS

Although content area teachers cannot be expected to teach remedial decoding skills, it is their responsibility to develop comprehension, extend vocabulary, and improve study skills.

Since the reading material of each content area has its own style and unique vocabulary, content area teachers must develop teaching methods appropriate to their particular discipline.

If content area teachers fail to make provisions for students who cannot decode or comprehend the assigned material, the students will derive nothing from the assignment and in addition will develop negative attitudes toward both the subject and toward reading in general. Teachers need to accommodate the reading differences among students by presenting the subject in a variety of ways: multileveled materials, nonprint materials, and class activities such as small group discussions. For a thorough discussion of content areas, see Chapters 5 and 6.

RECREATIONAL READING PROGRAMS

Recreational reading programs serve many purposes. First, students develop positive feelings toward reading. They are more likely to feel good about reading if self-selection and self-pacing is a part of the program. Second, recreational reading gives students practice in all reading skills. Third, students develop a taste for good literature when middle school libraries make available good preadolescent and adolescent literature. In short, recreational reading programs give students an opportunity to develop lifelong reading habits. A program of recreational reading is absolutely essential in a whole school reading program.

ORGANIZING THE READING PROGRAM

Middle schools may differ from one another in the way they are organized; therefore, organization of the reading program must differ also. Two hoped for characteristics of middle school organization are team teaching and large blocks of time. In middle schools still using a departmentalized organization, teachers can combine the reading program with the language arts program. This approach reduces the number of students teachers need to observe and increases the amount of time spent working with the students. For instance, instead of seeing 150 students in a separate subject approach, the teacher might have 75 to 90 students.

VALUE OF TEAM TEACHING

Team teaching exists when two or more teachers plan together and work together for the benefit of their students. Teaching teams can be interdisciplinary or oriented to a particular subject area. Interdisciplinary teams have teacher representatives from all major disciplines, with the team having complete responsibility for planning and implementing the instructional program for a group of students. Subject area teams have teachers from a single subject area share students during a block of time.

Advantages of team teaching include:

1. Teachers can provide for flexible grouping so more individualization can occur.
2. Teachers can make best use of student skills through peer tutoring.
3. Time can be better utilized so students have the time necessary for reading instruction.
4. Materials can be shared and thus be available to more students.

Middle schools that are organized into teaching teams can better meet the diverse needs of students. Once they have made decisions about the reading needs of their students, the team teachers can direct their efforts at meeting those needs throughout the school day.

GROPING WITH GROUPING

Some teachers feel that they can meet the reading needs of their students by subgrouping the large class on the basis of reading ability. Certainly, grouping within the class is superior to whole class instruction or ability grouping entire classes. But ability grouping of any kind does not narrow the range of abilities enough to ensure that the individual needs of students are met. Since many teachers recognize this and also realize the problems associated with ability grouping, they look for other alternatives. Some form of individualized reading program is usually the best solution.

DIAGNOSTIC/PRESCRIPTIVE ORGANIZATION FOR THE TEACHING OF READING SKILLS

Numerous commercial and teacher-developed checklists of skills, and accompanying tests, are being used in schools. The tests help teachers identify students' skill strengths and weaknesses, and teachers then prescribe activities that will develop the identified skill. Although this approach has something to offer the remedial reading teacher, it presents many problems for middle school language arts teachers.

Most of these systems are designed for the elementary student. Hours and hours are required to administer tests, record student profiles, and write prescriptions. Of course, middle school teachers should be familiar with students' reading development, but we do not recommend use of a reading system. Too much emphasis on specific skills can result in a fragmented reading program with too little attention devoted to practicing, applying, and enjoying reading.

SCHOOLWIDE ACTION PLAN

In every case, teachers need to be involved in the development of an action plan for the improvement of reading. If teachers are involved in the development of plans, they are much more likely to implement them. A reading committee should have a wide representation of teachers and be in constant touch with the entire faculty. No two middle school reading plans will be alike because the students, the physical resources, the personnel, and the material resources are different in each school.

A strong staff development program should be a part of the schoolwide action plan. Through staff development, teachers can become more aware of the needs of students and of ways to meet these needs. Together, in cooperative efforts, teachers can implement effective reading programs for their middle school students.

CHAPTER 3
THE REMEDIAL READERS

Teachers recognize many middle school students are frustrated by their inability to read materials appropriate for their age group. This group of frustrated readers offers the middle school staff one of its greatest challenges.

THE CHALLENGE OF THE REMEDIAL READERS

As a group, remedial readers in the middle school display the following characteristics: (1) insufficient decoding skills, (2) inadequate comprehension, (3) limited sight word vocabulary, (4) inability to read silently, (5) poor attitude toward reading, (6) feelings of "I cannot read," and (7) poor self-concept.

INSUFFICIENT DECODING SKILLS

Many remedial students are unable to decode words in materials at or near grade level. There is a range of ability here, from the virtual nonreader to the student who can decode or call words but not efficiently or with ease.

Teachers may be able to identify these difficulties through standardized tests. However, for zeroing in on specific problems, a criterion referenced test or a diagnostic reading test should be used. Informal reading inventories, as suggested by Potter and Rae[14], are of tremendous aid in pinpointing difficulties.

To determine if students can decode printed material, the teacher can select a one-hundred word passage and ask each student to read the material aloud. The student who miscalls no more than two or three words from the passage will probably be able to decode the material with little or no difficulty. If these selections are graded, the teachers can determine the reading grade level for the student. Graded material is available from commercial informal reading inventories such as Sivarolli's[20] or from graded basal reader selections. To determine specific decoding problems, the student is asked to read orally while the teacher records the types of errors the student makes. Oral reading errors or miscues can provide useful information about student decoding, especially if miscues are analyzed as suggested by Goodman[13].

Once teachers determine reading grade level and specific decoding problems, students can be provided with activities that help them overcome their general and specific difficulties with decoding. Spache[21] and Burmeister[5] suggest excellent activities designed to remediate decoding difficulties.

The following activities are designed for the student with decoding difficulties:

1. *Phrase flash cards* — We recommend the use of flash cards with entire phrases rather than single words so that sight words can be presented in a meaningful context.

2. *Writing stories* — Provide situations where the student writes or dictates stories. The words will be meaningful because the student wrote them, and that interest should motivate decoding.

3. *"Nym" games* — Games can be played using antonyms, homonyms, and synonyms. For example, form small teams of three students each and ask teams to come up with the most examples of antonyms, homonyms, or synonyms during a set period of time. Student interaction aids in building vocabulary.

4. *Prefix activities* — Fewer than twenty prefixes comprise over eighty percent of all words containing prefixes. (Prefixes used most often include *ex, un, in, pre, be, com,* and *re.*) Commercial and teacher-made activities such as matching games, word sheets, and prefix bingo can help students practice the use of prefixes.

5. *Suffix pantomime* — Have students act out different sets of suffixes. For example, with suffixes the word *big* becomes *bigger* or *biggest.* Encourage students to use comparative suffixes in a dramatization. This kind of activity often gives students a better understanding than written exercises can provide.

6. *Word ending game* — The most commonly used word endings include *ly, s, ed,* and *ment.* Demonstrate how these word endings are used in context. Blacken out the word endings in a newspaper or magazine article and ask students to supply the missing word endings.

7. *Word families* — Use phonograms or word families such as *hat, mat, sat.* Many programmed materials use word families, or you can make sliding card slotters, small pizza wheels, or puzzle pieces. After the students identify the words, ask them to write stories using these words.

8. *Word games* — Bingo or other sight word games are often used. Before deciding if these games are worthwhile the teacher must consider the time spent playing the game, the number of unknown words, and the effectiveness of the game.

INADEQUATE COMPREHENSION

Some students are able to pronounce words but cannot comprehend materials written at their grade level. Once teachers are certain that youngsters can decode a given selection, they can assess the level of comprehension.

There are several reliable procedures to measure comprehension. Teachers can ask students to discuss selections they have read. First ask for an overview of the passage, then ask specific questions about the selection. The questions should be interpretive as well as factual. If the student can answer at least six questions out of ten, the material is probably suitable for that student. If students are having difficulty comprehending what they read, the teacher should ask: What is the difficulty? Are students interested in the material? Were they reading the material for a particular purpose?

Comprehension is a complex area worthy of much attention. The following strategies are of interest to those teachers seeking to improve students' comprehension skills:

1. *Listen for the main idea* — For students who have trouble identifying main ideas, teachers can read short paragraphs from content area materials — the social studies book, for example. Progress from paragraphs where the main idea is

obvious to paragraphs where the main idea is imbedded. Reading aloud allows students to hear the ideas and avoids other reading problems. Students can be asked to read the paragraph at the conclusion of the exercise. The same procedure works for finding supporting ideas.

2. *Cloze exercises* — Make cloze exercises by deleting one or two words from a sentence written at the appropriate instructional level. For maximum effectiveness, choose sentences from newspaper articles, comics, and other high-interest selections. Black felt-tip pen can be used to obscure selected words when using a newspaper article. If sentences are retyped, make sure all deleted words are replaced by lines of equal length. For example: The pitcher _____ the ball to the third _____.

3. *Multileveled kits* — Multileveled kits offer materials on a wide range of reading levels and come complete with comprehension exercises. Most kits have simple directions for starting, maintaining, and evaluating students' progress in the materials. When using kits it is important for the teacher to confer with students on the amount of material read and the degree of comprehension. Many new kits are specifically designed for students who require low-level, high-interest material.

4. *Classifying games* — Classifying can be taught through commercial or teacher-made games that help students identify main ideas. Teachers can start with simple pictures of automobiles and ask students to classify cars as foreign or domestic. Students move on to word cards and classify things like fruits and vegetables. When students can classify simple objects, they can progress to classifying phrases.

5. *Sequence activities* — Comic strips provide sequencing exercises that are inexpensive and interesting. Cover the comic strip with clear Contact paper, then cut out each individual comic picture. Ask students to place the pictures in logical order. Students may assemble a comic strip in an order that is different from the original, but so long as the conversation is logical, the activity has served the purpose of getting students to think about correct sequence.

6. *High-interest, low-vocabulary workbooks* — Several companies publish workbooks of this type. Workbooks can be used as

designed or can serve as a springboard to many individual activities. Activities on single or double pages are more likely to interest students because they can be completed in a short time. One workbook can yield numerous activities, and if two workbooks are used no pages are lost in mounting. An answer key should be available for self-checking.

7. *Individual conferences* — As with peer tutoring, human interaction yields high returns in comprehension development. A teacher's questions and reinforcement can help a student greatly improve thinking comprehension.

8. *Peer tutoring* — Many students just need to hear other students explain how they arrived at right answers. By hearing verbal accounts of another person's ways of solving or understanding, students can improve their own comprehension.

9. *Small group interaction* — Provide opportunities for discussion and interation. Students' thinking becomes clearer when they hear another person's point of view on selected topics or issues.

LIMITED SIGHT WORD VOCABULARY

Remedial readers in the middle school often have some decoding skills but are handicapped by a limited sight vocabulary. Teachers might become aware of this handicap by listening when students read aloud on an individual basis. Alternately, teachers may administer an individual sight word list such as the Dolch Basic Sight Word List[7] or the Fry Instant Words[10]. Tests such as these can be administered to a group, with the teacher asking students to circle the listed words as they are pronounced. However, if time permits, the individual method of administering sight word tests is superior.

There are many ways for teachers to help students improve their sight word vocabulary. Here are a few suggestions:

1. *Checkers* — Make checkerboards and write a word on each square. The game is played like checkers, but before players can place checkers on a new square, they must pronounce the word on that square.

2. *Dominoes* — Make word dominoes by dividing index cards

into two parts and writing a word on each half. Use each word more than once. Play the game like regular dominoes; to make a move, students match words that are the same.

3. *Bingo* — The game is played like regular bingo with word cards divided into twenty-five squares. A word is written in each square. Students cover the word with a marker as someone pronounces it.

4. *Football* — Make a cardboard football field with lines indicating 10 yards, and add a cardboard football. Make sight word cards and place them face up. A student who correctly identifies a word advances the ball 10 yards. An incorrect identification means a penalty, so the player goes backward 10 yards. The play is similar to football; the winner is the student who moves all the way down the board.

INABILITY TO READ SILENTLY

Some students cannot read silently or do so with difficulty. The alert teacher can spot these students reading aloud very softly or forming the words with their lips when asked to read silently. These readers often have problems with comprehension and of course read slowly. Many reading programs emphasize oral reading, and this may contribute to the problem; children receive little, if any, practice in silent reading.

How can teachers help students improve silent reading skills? The following techniques have been successful:

1. *Chewing gum* — Students who read softly to themselves or move their lips when reading often have difficulty breaking this habit. Youngsters who chew gum or put a pencil in their mouth are made aware that their lips are moving. This is a first step to breaking the habit.

2. *Books with audiotapes* — Listening to tapes that accompany books can help students read without moving their lips. The tapes save readers the task of sounding out the words, and often subvocalizing disappears.

3. *Read, read, and read* — The best possible remedy is practice. Most students who read often on an independent level stop reading orally and subvocally.

POOR ATTITUDE TOWARD READING

Middle schoolers who do not read well generally dislike reading. This negative attitude is usually bolstered by grading practices and the verbal and nonverbal behavior of teachers, family, and peers. Informal inventories of reading interests and reading attitudes can be used to identify these students, who avoid reading whenever they can. It is not easy to help students overcome poor attitudes, but the following suggestions can be successful:

1. *Work together* — Middle school students are greatly influenced by their peers; therefore, having a fellow student with a good attitude toward reading work with a reader who has a poor attitude is very effective. In most cases a peer tutor can bring about change much faster than a teacher.

2. *Something fun* — Students who are given opportunities to choose their own reading materials usually choose materials meaningful to them. Offer choices covering a wide range of interest and readability, and ask students to make their own selections.

FEELINGS OF "I CANNOT READ"

Some students not only have a negative attitude toward reading but are convinced that they cannot learn to read. Most remedial readers in the middle school have developed these feelings. It is a challenge to provide remedial readers with opportunities for success. You could try these approaches:

1. *Language experience stories* — Demonstrate to the student that she or he can read something: ask the student to dictate a story and then read it back. Students who experience small successes often enough will soon realize that they can read. In order to be successful this type of remediation must occur on an individual basis.

2. *Confidence conferences* — Teachers need to have individual conferences with students to convey their confidence in each student's learning potential. Many students have been "bottle fed" so long they are unaware the responsibility for

learning to read is their own. Once they accept the responsibility for learning to read, they just may do something about it.

POOR SELF-CONCEPT

Poor readers have difficulty developing healthy self-concepts because schools and society place such a high premium on being able to read. Many poor readers question their value as human beings. While there are inventories such as the Coopersmith[6] to assess self-concept or self-esteem, sensitive teachers can usually spot students with a low opinion of themselves. Here are a few suggestions for helping students improve self-concept:

1. *Reading with younger students* — One of the best ways to increase students' self-esteem is to have them help younger students read. Low achievers can help younger students so long as they know just a little bit more than the younger ones. The tutors should experience a surge of self-confidence because they achieve status with the younger students.

2. *Proving your worth* — All middle school students need to prove their worth, but especially those with low self-concepts. Volunteer activities, in no way related to reading, can make students feel worthwhile and can have a positive effect upon reading achievement. For instance, you might ask students to make table decorations for a home for the elderly.

3. *Excellent at anything* — Most students in any middle school can do something well. If students do not seem to excel at something, it is probably because they have never been given a chance to do so. The student who can catch fifteen pennies flipped from the elbows should receive attention just as the student who can hop fastest on one foot. Youngsters should have opportunities to excel in non-academic areas.

4. *Choices make for success* — If the only option given students is to read a 300-page book, certain students will perform poorly. If there are many choices, ranging from reading several short articles to reading an entire book, more students will

experience success with the assignment and thus feel good about themselves.

READING APPROACHES APPROPRIATE FOR MIDDLE SCHOOL REMEDIAL READERS

Middle school teachers can choose among many different approaches to reading instruction for remedial readers: (1) individualized reading, (2) language experience, (3) basal reading, (4) programmed reading, and (5) an eclectic or combined approach.

INDIVIDUALIZED READING

In an individualized program students select their own reading materials and pace themselves. Teacher-student conferences provide opportunities to discuss trade books or other extra-curricular materials the student is reading. During conferences they also work on skill development when it is appropriate to do so. Both teacher and student keep records of conferences, noting the strengths and needs of the student.

Barbe and Abbott[2] present many practical ideas regarding individualized or personalized programs. They emphasize that in addition to the actual teaching of reading, a reading program must develop the student's love for reading.

Teachers who favor the individualized approach feel its major strength is that students are reading materials interesting to them and appropriate to their level. Student-teacher conferences usually last from three to ten minutes and are scheduled at least twice per week. The high degree of personal attention given each student seems to motivate readers and build self-confidence.

One drawback of the individualized approach is the amount of time required to conduct conferences and keep individual records. Then, too, many teachers feel they must read a book before they can conduct a conference. This need not be an obstacle, however. By scanning the book during the conference, a teacher can ask meaningful questions about characters, plot, and setting without having read the entire book.

Although individualized reading is an excellent way to motivate the remedial reader, the teacher must make extra efforts to find reading materials easy enough yet sufficiently interesting to hold the attention of middle school students.

LANGUAGE EXPERIENCE

The language experience approach encourages students to talk about what they are thinking. The teacher builds upon oral language skills by allowing students to dictate or write their thoughts on paper.

Allen[1] suggests that this approach helps students realize the interrelationship among reading, writing, speaking, listening, and thinking. A major advantage of the language experience approach is that the reading materials are meaningful to the reader since the words are derived from the student's own experience. Critics of the approach point out that since the reading materials are those written by the reader, there is scant opportunity to develop new ideas through reading.

Although the language experience approach can be valuable, the process is quite time consuming if the student cannot write and therefore must dictate to the teacher. If dictation is necessary, try using a teacher aide, volunteer, cross-age tutor, or peer tutor to record the dictated stories.

BASAL READING

Basal readers are sets of books containing reading selections graded in difficulty. Specific skills are introduced and sequenced according to the philosophy of the writers and editors. The teacher's guides contain suggestions for teaching and offer a rationale for the approach. Most basal readers are accompanied by workbooks and other supplementary materials.

If basal readers are used in a middle school remedial reading program, they should not be followed page by page with accompanying workbooks. Often the basal reader spells failure for the student who has known only failure with basals. Students should not be reading from basals used in previous grades, even though they may be appropriate to the students' reading levels.

Oral reading of basals is valuable for purposes of diagnosis and for sharing. Although some teachers are strong believers in oral reading, too much oral reading can be harmful. Remedial readers benefit most when the oral readers are good readers. If poor readers share orally, they should practice first and read only short selections.

PROGRAMMED READING

Programmed reading materials present learning content in small steps and provide immediate reinforcement of a student's response. An advantage of programmed reading is that students can proceed at their own rates. One disadvantage is that remedial students may get frustrated if their progress is slow.

THE ECLECTIC OR COMBINED APPROACH

There is no one best method to teach reading to remedial readers. Teachers who are successful use several methods, selecting the most appropriate ones for each student.

Some say that the eclectic approach is a "cop out" and that teachers cannot function under this system. Granted, it is not easy to use several approaches, and teachers must understand the reading process, be well versed in materials and approaches, be proficient in assessing students' needs, and be organized in managing materials and records.

A teacher using an eclectic approach uses one or more approaches best suited to the learning style of a particular student. For example, the teacher observes that Sarah, a remedial reader, does not seem to be making much progress with a programmed reading approach, so the teacher decides to try a combination of language experience and individualized reading. These two approaches, along with peer tutoring, prove to be very effective.

Several variables influence the number of approaches used: (1) the learning needs of the students, (2) the quality and quantity of materials available to the teacher, (3) the management skills and expertise of the teacher, and (4) the number of students in the class. Teachers need to remember that differences among remedial readers are probably as striking as differences between remedial and accelerated readers, and therefore they should exercise caution in assessing remedial readers and implementing instructional strategies. Experience, interest, and staff development help teachers become more confident in their ability to use the eclectic approach.

Attitude is important, too. Teachers need to be on guard against their own negative thoughts — that students cannot or will not read. When teachers believe that students cannot learn to read, their suspicions will probably be confirmed. Remedial readers have failed often and they need teachers who believe that they will succeed. Teachers who perceive remedial readers in positive ways are headed in the right direction. While teaching expertise is important, caring and enthusiasm are equally vital.

CHAPTER 4
THE ON GRADE LEVEL READER
AND THE ACCELERATED READER

On grade level readers are those students who have little difficulty reading materials typically aimed at their current grade level. Accelerated readers are excellent readers, competent with materials designed for students in grades higher than their own. Though both groups still have reading needs, many times these on grade level and accelerated readers become lost in the crowd because their reading abilities seem in step with grade level reading demands.

The on grade level and accelerated middle school readers have few or no decoding problems with the exception of some new and difficult words or proper nouns. Since these students have no serious problems with comprehension, it is difficult to identify their specific strengths and weaknesses. However both groups require some direct reading instruction aimed at meeting the following needs: (1) need for better comprehension, (2) need for a wider and more varied vocabulary, (3) need for improved study skills, (4) need to increase flexibility of rate, and (5) need to do more recreational reading.

NEED FOR BETTER COMPREHENSION

Readers who have excellent decoding skills may still experience difficulty comprehending. Middle schoolers need to comprehend at three levels: literal, interpretive, and evaluative. As one teacher put it, students need to be able to read the line, read between the lines, and read beyond the lines. Students who are accustomed to literal or factual questions may have difficulty answering questions at the interpretive and evaluative levels. For ideas about various levels of questions, see Sanders[19].

Teachers can use several methods to determine the comprehension abilities of on grade level students. They can have students read a selected passage and then ask them questions written at each of the three levels. Further, if teachers wish to know if students will be able to comprehend a particular textbook, we recommend they construct and administer a cloze test. (See Chapter 5 for further information regarding this test.)

To improve comprehension of on grade level and accelerated readers, you might try one or more of the activities outlined below:

1. *Multileveled kits* — Multileveled kits are available for developmental reading programs at the middle school level. Students at different levels can work on materials from the same kit. Teachers should exercise caution with kits to ensure that students do not become bored.

2. *Comprehension folder activities* — Teachers can make inexpensive and effective activities by mounting interesting articles or short stories from newspapers or magazines in file folders. Include cards with questions about the selections. File folders store easily, are durable, and are a good investment in time and effort for the middle school teacher.

3. *Comprehension task cards* — Teachers can obtain task cards that contain high-interest, low-vocabulary stories and questions about the stories. These cards may be used with pairs of students to keep interest high. Teachers can make their own activity cards for comprehension by pasting a story on a card and writing several questions about the story.

4. *Newspaper main idea hunt* — Choose interesting news items from newspapers, and ask students to underline the main ideas in each paragraph. Several copies of the same issue of the newspaper provide enough materials for a small group activity.

NEED FOR A WIDER AND MORE VARIED VOCABULARY

On grade level and accelerated students often need to increase their reading vocabulary and add to the richness of their language. Limited vocabulary can be the result of a home environment where vocabulary is meager and where parents do very little voluntary reading. Teachers can assess students' vocabulary by observing their writing, by listening to their oral language, and by being aware of their ability to define words.

Instructional strategies designed to improve vocabulary include:

1. *Finding multiple meanings* — Students take simple words such as *sign, check,* and *type* and write as many meanings for the words as they can. Allowing students to work with a buddy is a good system. After the students have listed multiple meanings for the selected words, they can list other words with multiple meanings.

2. *Adjective brainstorming* — Students think of all the adjectives that are related to certain nouns, such as *dog, sky,* or *flowers.* Students work in pairs and needn't defend their choices.

3. *Cinquain, haiku, tanka, and diamante* — All of these creative forms of poetry are useful in developing vocabulary. (Most language arts methods books have detailed descriptions of these writing forms.) Writing these types of poetry may be a group effort. Triads, for instance, can be composed by a small group.

4. *Alphabet brainstorming* — Students go through the alphabet, writing the first words that come to mind for each letter of the alphabet. Students can work in pairs or in threes, and the rules can vary. For instance, students can see how many times they can proceed through the alphabet in a fifteen-minute period, or they can list three words for each letter, or record only five-letter words.

5. *Making words* — An old party game that works with middle schoolers involves giving students letter combinations and asking them to form as many words as they can from the combination. Be sure the seed word contains enough vowels so that several words can be spelled from it. Vary the rules to allow students to add letters to form new words, or restrict students to words of three or four letters.

6. *Mystery words* — Form the class into several groups and instruct each student within the group to browse through a magazine to find three words new to them that they think no one else in the group knows. The student writes each word on a separate card. Dictionaries should be available. Each student will show one card to the group to see if anyone in the group knows the word. After the meaning is checked in the dictionary, the next student presents a card. A point is given for each known word.

7. *Crossword puzzles* — Crossword puzzles from the newspaper or from puzzle books can provide an excellent vocabulary exercise. Many students enjoy composing their own crossword puzzles to be used by other students.

8. *Synonym fun* — Students look up ten common words in the thesaurus and then write a silly story using the more difficult synonyms for those words. Students can work in pairs and share their stories with another pair of students.

9. *Obsolete words* — Students make lists of words no longer in use, getting tips from parents and other adults. Alongside these obsolete words, write words that are commonly used in their place today. This is a good team activity and stimulates much interest in vocabulary development.

10. *Listing sexist words* — Middle schoolers enjoy finding those words in their vocabularies based on the word *man,* for instance. Students today are aware of sexist language and many delight in making lists.

11. *Regional or dialect dictionary* — Students enjoy developing dictionaries of words common to one particular region or dialect. Every part of the country has words that are unique to that region. Middle school students can usually think of some words, but this is a good activity in which to involve adults.

12. *Slang dictionary* — Middle schoolers love slang and are usually delighted to have the opportunity to develop a slang dictionary. (It is important to emphasize the difference between slang and profanity.) This is a good small group activity.

NEED FOR IMPROVED STUDY SKILLS

Students must acquire study skills if they are to become independent learners. Major task areas include locating information, organizing information, and using graphic aids. Within these task areas are included several specific study skills — for example, using an appendix, using an encyclopedia, and using a glossary.

Many middle schoolers who read without serious problems desperately need to improve their study habits. Teachers can determine if students possess good study habits by observing their work and by administering informal inventories constructed to assess skills in this area. Helping students analyze their current study habits is a first step toward developing good habits. The following inventory helps students identify present habits and indicates to the teacher and the students student learning preferences. The inventory can be modified to meet particular needs by including or excluding certain items.

STUDY SKILLS INVENTORY
HOW I LIKE TO STUDY

	Like Me	Not Like Me
1. I don't like to check my own work.		
2. I study best in the morning.		
3. I like to choose my assignments.		
4. I like assignments that I do myself rather than those done in a group.		
5. I like writing but I don't like reading.		
6. I like daily assignments rather than week-long assignments.		
7. I wait until the last minute to finish my assignments.		
8. I enjoy drawing.		
9. I don't plan my work very well.		
10. I study best at night.		
11. I like to finish my work on time.		
12. I don't like to use the library.		
13. I like to make things as part of my lessons.		
14. I want to finish my work at school.		
15. I would rather work in a group than work alone.		
16. I study best in the afternoon.		
17. I can find anything I want in the library.		
18. I like to check my own work.		
19. I organize my time well.		
20. I don't mind reading but I hate writing.		

There are many ways to teach students good study skills. Experienced teachers have had success with these methods:

1. *Fun with following directions* — Students work in pairs to write directions for simple activities such as making a paper airplane. After students complete the writing, they exchange directions with another pair of students and carry out the directions. This exercise helps youngsters learn to follow printed directions on packages, instructions included with kits, and step-by-step science experiments.

2. *Oral note taking* — Some students have difficulty deciding what ideas should be written down when making notes on written material. A good exercise starts with the students reading a few simple paragraphs aloud. After discussing what the students think is important for note writing, they write their ideas on the chalkboard. This note taking activity is followed with a written activity.

3. *Library orientation* — Many middle schoolers need to become more aware of the resources of the school library in order to fully utilize its facilities. The content of an orientation session will depend upon the knowledge and experience that the students already demonstrate. Avoid lecture sessions; it is usually best to follow a brief introduction with exercises that require students to actually find information or practice other library skills. For instance, to teach the use of the biographical dictionary, ask students to find several actual biographies. Many librarians will prepare interesting exercises.

NEED TO INCREASE FLEXIBILITY OF RATE

It is important that readers are able to read different materials at different rates. Many on grade level and accelerated readers read all materials at the same rate rather than adjust the rate as appropriate. Teachers need to provide opportunities for these students to gain flexibility in reading rate. The observant teacher can determine whether students vary reading rate to fit the type of material and the purpose for reading.

Two strategies have been shown effective in speeding up reading rate:

1. *Speed reading devices* — Teachers might use devices such as tachistoscopes, controlled machines, and reading pacers. Tachistoscopes present printed materials for brief periods of time. Controlled machines use projectors to project reading materials at varying speeds. Reading pacers have extensions or arms that move over a printed page from top to bottom at different regulated rates.
2. *Timed exercises* — Teachers might select passages and time students to determine reading rates. Students can then work to improve their rates on these passages. Speed can be charted on graphs so students can see their progress. Teachers need to be sure that comprehension levels are maintained as speed increases.

NEED TO DO MORE RECREATIONAL READING

It is important for students to appreciate and enjoy good literature. Just because on grade level and accelerated students are able to read does not mean that they will read for pleasure. Why not? Perhaps they are kept busy reading assigned materials or have no adult models who read for pleasure. Some may be turned off because they have to write or give book reports on everything they read.

Teachers may discover students' recreational reading habits by asking them to complete appropriate inventories; however, caution should be exercised here since some students will respond the way they think teachers want them to respond. Observing students' reading habits and discussing with them books that they have read usually yields the best information. Refer to Chapter 7 for strategies that will help teachers increase the amount of recreational reading done by their students.

READING APPROACHES APPROPRIATE FOR ON GRADE LEVEL AND ACCELERATED READERS

We believe developmental reading instruction is necessary for on grade level and accelerated readers if their reading potential is to be fully realized. Of course, these readers do not need the same amount or type of reading instruction as remedial readers, but many are still in need of some instruction. We are not advocating a basal reading series or any other specific approach; however, we believe that reading instruction should occur several times per week, depending on the needs of the students. It is best to designate instructional time, because unless time is allocated for an activity it often does not occur.

A developmental program is one where attention is given to the development of reading in a planned and systematic way. The program will not be the same for all students because their needs are so divergent. Some approaches appropriate for the on grade level middle schooler include individualized reading with trade books or basals, and an eclectic or combined approach. For accelerated readers, basals are not appropriate.

INDIVIDUALIZED READING

Please refer to Chapter 3 for a discussion of the individualized reading approach. This approach is well suited to on grade level and accelerated readers since motivation is high and growth is thus facilitated.

Chapter 3 also contains a section on basal reading. Teachers can use basal readers with on grade level readers, but students should be allowed to self-select and pace themselves through the literature selections. The teachers' guides provide helpful ideas for teaching students who have demonstrated particular needs.

ECLECTIC OR COMBINED READING

The eclectic or combined reading approach is discussed in Chapter 3. Of course, the methods used with on grade level and accelerated readers are different from those used with remedial readers. Teachers match student needs with appropriate materials, so that no one approach or material is used exclusively with all students. The number of approaches and materials in use depends upon available resources, student needs, teacher experience, and so forth.

READING IN THE LITERATURE PROGRAM

In some middle schools the only material available is the literature textbook, and some teachers try to meet students' reading needs through the literature program. Although the teaching of literature can be a valid approach to the teaching of reading, sad to say it often is the only reading instruction some students receive. Teachers need to be certain that students can read the literature textbook. Do not assume that all selections are on the same reading level, since level of difficulty can vary from one selection to the next.

When using the textbook, teachers need to observe students' reading behaviors, note needs, and provide appropriate instruction to meet those needs. Proper use of questioning techniques can improve comprehension. The literature book, if used properly, can help develop students' vocabulary, spark interest in certain topics, and facilitate recreational reading in those areas.

IN CONCLUSION

Teachers must challenge on grade level and accelerated readers and be challenged by them. Teachers need to "take the ceiling off" and let students progress at their own rate. But teachers cannot remove the floor. In other words, there is a continuing need for reading instruction if students are to make progress and become better and better readers.

CHAPTER 5
READING IN THE BIG FOUR —
ENGLISH, SOCIAL STUDIES,
SCIENCE, AND MATH

Students make much progress between the recognition of their first word and the time they become a mature reader. At each step along the way reading instruction should be different, with goals and activities tailored to accommodate students' changing needs and interests. Many middle school students are making progress in reading, but most still need help in becoming mature readers.

It is frequently said that every teacher is a teacher of reading. Of course, each content area teacher needn't be a teacher of reading in a remedial sense. But content area teachers need to understand the reading process and be able to note students' strengths and weaknesses as readers. Also teachers need to present printed materials in such a way that students understand the content presented and can grow in their reading abilities.

Reading in content areas is a big mystery to some teachers. It needn't be. Reading instruction here as elsewhere is based on good common teaching sense and able teachers have been and are already doing many of the activities recommended here. While Miss Gertrude Horst (one of our favorite history teachers, retired) and thousands like her may not be able to give names to the activities discussed here, she and other teachers were in fact making these activities a part of daily teaching long before it was vogue to do so. Miss Horst, a bright and caring person, exhibited common sense and great sensitivity to the needs of students, and these attitudes guided all her teaching practices.

Content area teachers are the best "teachers of reading" for their own subject areas because of the following characteristics:

1. Their enthusiasm for the subject sets a purpose and helps motivate students to read the material.
2. Their understanding of the content enables them to identify the key concepts students should learn from the printed materials.

3. Their knowledge of the vocabulary helps facilitate students' vocabulary growth.
4. Their awareness of resources to use in teaching the content provides alternate ways to help students learn.

SKILLS OF CONTENT AREA TEACHERS

To do a good job, content area teachers need to possess eight skills related to reading. Teachers should be able to —

1. Use successful techniques for teaching vocabulary in their own content area.
2. Assist students in improving comprehension.
3. Determine if students can comprehend reading materials, using procedures such as the cloze.
4. Assist students in becoming flexible in their reading rates.
5. Guide reading assignments.
6. Assist students with study techniques.
7. Determine the reading level of a book using a formula such as the Fry Readability Graph.
8. Accommodate the needs of remedial readers in the content area.

SKILL ONE: USE SUCCESSFUL TECHNIQUES FOR TEACHING VOCABULARY IN THEIR OWN CONTENT AREA

Teachers are generally expert in the specialized vocabulary of their own content area, and therefore they are the best ones to teach that vocabulary. Asking students to do pencil and paper type activities is not a satisfactory way to extend vocabulary, nor is it helpful to assign fifteen or twenty isolated words each week. Vocabulary growth is best accomplished within the context of each content area. Students' reading vocabularies are limited by their previous word range. To build vocabulary, teachers can provide opportunities for students to experience new concepts; to add to their awareness of vocabulary teachers can use new words and encourage much verbal interaction.

Because students' vocabularies differ so greatly, content area teachers will find it impossible to teach every student every word in a particular reading assignment. Before teaching any new words, teachers should determine which words are not known by a majority of the students. A simple test in matching vocabulary can help here. Be selective and choose only those words necessary for understanding. Proper nouns or foreign words which students will seldom encounter in their reading should receive less emphasis.

There are several categories of words that students often do not know:

1. Words used in speaking but not in reading
2. Words with geographic meanings
3. Words with scientific and technical meanings
4. Words of a general nature that take on different meanings in different content areas
5. Words that have ambiguous meanings
6. Words that are obsolete.

Students learn vocabulary in many different ways, just as they have individualized styles for learning other information. It is the responsibility of the content area teachers to help each student develop a strategy that meets that student's needs.

SKILL TWO: ASSIST STUDENTS IN IMPROVING COMPREHENSION

One of the primary goals of education is to develop students' thinking processes. Teachers should keep this goal in mind as they work to produce independent learners who can comprehend and evaluate what they read. Comprehension of printed materials is a thinking process, and as students mature in their thought processes they display greater reading comprehension.

Reading comprehension can be described on three or four different levels:

- Literal level — The lowest level of comprehension is concerned with recall of facts, sequence, enumeration.
- Interpretive level — This level goes beyond the literal level. The reader makes generalizations, see relationships such as cause and effect, makes comparisons.

- Critical level — At this level, the reader evaluates and judges information. The author's presentation, accuracy, and truthfulness are examined.
- Creative level — The reader becomes involved with the author's information and integrates it into his or her own thinking.

Content area teachers can help students learn to think and comprehend at the various levels. Too often, the questions teachers ask and the activities they assign, both written and oral, are at the literal, factual level. Good teachers work very hard to structure questions and develop assignments that will encourage students to think interpretively, critically, and creatively. All middle school teachers need to examine their own questioning skills and work on the art of higher level questioning.

An important part of comprehension is learning to identify main ideas. Often the teaching of this skill is left to the language arts teacher, when in fact each content area teacher should be working with students in this regard. Teachers often assume that students have learned how to locate main ideas early in their reading instruction. They forget that the skill must be refined as students move from easier to more difficult reading material.

Students' abilities to outline and summarize — to read effectively and organize the ideas they read — are dependent upon their being able to identify main ideas. Workbook exercises are not a particularly good way to teach this skill because students may still have difficulty transferring the skill to content area reading. Instead, let students practice finding the main ideas in paragraphs taken from regular content area lessons.

SKILL THREE: DETERMINE IF STUDENTS CAN COMPREHEND READING MATERIALS

How do content area teachers determine students' reading strengths and needs? Chapter 2 contains a section on this subject; however, some of the methods mentioned there are more appropriate for language arts and reading teachers. Any information about students' reading abilities should be reported to the content area teachers on forms similar to the ones suggested in Chapter 2. To be effective and useful, the form must be simple.

Cloze Procedure

The cloze procedure is one method of determining whether students can comprehend certain written material. Bormuth[3] developed this procedure which can be administered easily and provides valuable information. To develop a cloze test, the teacher selects a representative passage of 250 words from a textbook (or similar material) and types the passage deleting every fifth word and leaving blank spaces of equal length for each deleted word. Each student receives a copy of the passage and is asked to fill in the blanks. To be correct the student must supply the exact word deleted. Each correct response counts for two percentage points. To determine the student's reading level for the passage, use the following scale developed by Bormuth:

> 58 – 100% correct — Independent level
> 44 – 57% correct — Instructional level
> 0 – 43% correct — Frustration level

The beginning of a cloze passage might look like this:

Each year there are _____(1)_____ crocodiles on the face _____(2)_____ the earth. The American _____(3)_____ is one of 21 _____(4)_____ . It is estimated that _____(5)_____ have been in existence _____(6)_____ 200 million years. There _____(7)_____ laws to protect the _____(8)_____ .

Before Checking Comprehension

Students cannot comprehend printed materials if they cannot decode the words. Teachers need to be sure students can decode before assuming there is a comprehension difficulty. A procedure for determining whether a student can decode was described in Chapter 3. Briefly, on a one-to-one basis, the teacher asks a student to read orally from a 100-word passage selected from a textbook. The teacher keeps a record of words the student miscalls, and this gives a valid indication of reading level:

> 0 words missed — Independent level
> 1–4 words missed — Instructional level
> 5 or more words missed — Frustration level

If students are at the independent or instructional level, they can decode the material. If they score at the frustration level, do not expect them to succeed with that book.

SKILL FOUR: ASSIST STUDENTS IN BECOMING FLEXIBLE IN THEIR READING RATES

Mature readers do not read every word. Reading every word makes for a slow and inefficient reader at the middle school level. Middle school students need to learn to adjust their reading rates to the material and according to their purposes for reading. Content area teachers can help students become aware of ways to increase or decrease reading rates:

- *Scanning* — Reading to find an answer in a passage
- *Skimming* — Reading to gain an impression of the content
- *Rapid reading* — Reading for the main idea(s)
- *Study reading* — Reading to gain familiarity with content in textbooks or similar material
- *Careful reading* — Reading to analyze as in math problems or scientific formulas.

Students should learn to ask themselves the following questions to determine how fast they should read: (1) How difficult is the material? (2) Why am I reading the material? and (3) How much do I already know about the content? Middle schoolers who evaluate reading materials in this way are more efficient readers.

SKILL FIVE: GUIDE READING ASSIGNMENTS

The guided reading lesson or directed reading activity are essentially the same and are designed for students who read at their instructional level, not for those at the independent or frustration levels. Usually the procedure is used with small groups or with whole class reading assignments since it is difficult or impossible for a teacher to spend so much time with an individual student. The steps for a guided reading assignment are as follows:

1. Build up the students' range of experience so they can

the class studies poetry, at a later date, the students locate poetry inspired by the Pyrenees Mountains.

SKILL SIX: ASSIST STUDENTS WITH STUDY TECHNIQUES, SUCH AS SQ3R

There are numerous study techniques that give students an organized way to get the most from what they read. Middle school students can profit from study techniques, and teachers who use these techniques feel they improve students' understanding of textbook content.

One rather simple technique is the SQ3R (Survey, Question, Read, Recite, and Review), developed by Francis P. Robinson[15]. Teachers can follow the technique as described below, or modify it to suit particular needs.

- *Survey* — The student reads to get an idea of what a chapter or section is about. Usually the introduction, the summary, and the first sentence of each paragraph are read carefully. Students are encouraged to glance at any pictures or graphic materials. As a result of this quick glance, the student begins to develop a purpose for reading the selection.

- *Question* — The student develops questions from chapter subheadings by changing the subheadings into questions. Students should formulate no more than three questions for each subheading. This may sound like a difficult step, but many content area textbooks are organized in such a way that it is easy to accomplish this procedure.

- *Read* — Students read the content to find answers to the questions they have developed. Since their questions correspond to subheadings, it is easy to locate the answers.

- *Recite* — Students restate the content in their own words after they find the answers to their questions.

- *Review* — Students can review, either orally or in writing, each section of the chapter. Again students are thinking about the answers to questions formulated in Step 2, and additionally, any other information found in their reading.

We offer one word of caution about using a study technique like SQ3R. The first time around, students may become discouraged because it takes so much time to use the method. To minimize this problem, teachers might suggest students begin with short chapters or portions of chapters. Furthermore, students should be encouraged to develop their own study style by adapting any study technique to meet their own needs. Students should not be required to hand in formal assignments based on study techniques since these methods are designed for their own benefit. Brief, sketchy questions and answers may be sufficient.

SKILL SEVEN: DETERMINE THE READING LEVEL OF A BOOK WITH A FORMULA SUCH AS THE FRY READABILITY GRAPH

Content area textbooks are sometimes written at a higher level of readability than that indicated by the publisher. For this reason teachers need to determine the reading level of textbooks before they purchase or select them for student use.

There are numerous readability formulas in use. We recommend the Fry[11] Readability Graph, included on the following page.

SKILL EIGHT: ACCOMMODATE THE NEEDS OF REMEDIAL READERS IN THE CONTENT AREAS

Most teachers are aware that they need to plan for the remedial readers in their classes, but it is not always an easy task. Some of the students (the poorer readers) cannot read the textbook and other materials used in their class. This problem is magnified because many content area textbooks are written as much as two or three notches above the grade for which they are intended. Thus the textbook is out of reach or very difficult for not only the remedial readers but also for many on grade level readers. To be effective, teachers need to know the actual readability levels of materials they use, and they need to assess, through such procedures as the cloze, each student's ability to read and comprehend the materials.

Of course, content area teachers cannot assume the role of remedial reading teachers. However, content area teachers can provide alternate ways for remedial readers to learn the content. Parallel textbooks written for the low level readers may be available. A suggested list of materials parallel in content, but written at a lower reading level, is found in the teacher's edition

GRAPH FOR ESTIMATING READABILITY*

By Edward Fry, Rutgers University Reading Center,
New Brunswick, New Jersey

Average number of syllables per 100 words

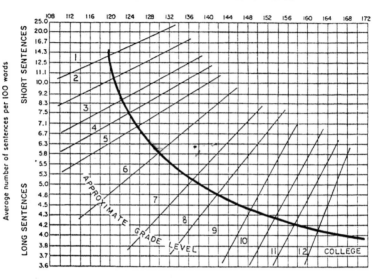

Directions: Randomly select three 100-word passages from a
book or an article. Plot the average number of syllables and the average number of sentences per 100
words on the graph to determine the grade level of
the material. Choose more passages per book if
great variability is observed, and conclude that the
book has uneven readability. Few books will fall in
the gray area, but when they do, grade level scores
are invalid.

Example:

	Syllables	Sentences
1st Hundred Words	124	6.6
2nd Hundred Words	141	5.5
3rd Hundred Words	158	6.8
AVERAGE	141	6.3

Readability: 7th Grade (see dot plotted on graph)

* For further information and validity data, see the April 1968 *Journal of Reading*
and the March 1969 *Reading Teacher*.

of some textbooks. Some teachers tear apart lower elementary level textbooks and reconstruct them into mini-units. Other teachers have rewritten textbooks at a lower readability level; however, because of the time involved, it is unreasonable to expect teachers to undertake this job unless they are paid for the extra work. Some teachers read textbooks onto audiotape or record someone else reading the textbook.

It is important to remember that low level readers, who work in materials different from the better readers, often feel a stigma. Teachers need to do everything possible to minimize these negative feelings.

SPECIFIC CONTENT AREAS

The following discussion deals with several reading issues as they relate to specific areas of the curriculum. See the Bibliography for additional suggestions of books that focus on teaching reading in the content areas.

SCIENCE

Even when science is taught in a laboratory environment, students need to refer to their science textbook. In order to read a science text, the student must be able to handle the specialized vocabulary, follow directions, read graphic aids, visualize content from the printed page, see cause-effect relationships, and understand various scientific writing patterns.

Preparation is very important here. Students cannot understand written material if they lack the necessary background experience. For some units of study, the actual preparation or building of background experience may take up more time than the actual reading.

Science teachers often use a guided reading activity format when they make reading assignments. Science materials contain much specialized vocabulary; teachers need to be selective and teach students only those words essential for understanding the content.

Science content often includes figures, mathematical quotations, or directions, and students are expected to make generalizations and understand details. Reading rate is usually slow;

however, this varies according to the writing style, the learners' familiarity with the material, and the purpose for reading.

According to Robinson[16], six main patterns of writing are (1) enumeration, (2) classification, (3) generalization, (4) problem solving, (5) comparison or contrast, and (6) sequence. Most students, including good readers, need assistance in identifying these patterns. Science teachers can help students get the most out of their reading assignments by providing necessary background information and by guiding scientific reading.

- *Enumeration* — Many facts are listed with few cues to the reader as to main ideas and subtopics. Outlining and other activities will help the student isolate the topic, subtopic, and details.

- *Classification* — Topics are usually divided into parts with subtopics, requiring students to determine similarities and differences. Students often find it helpful to make charts.

- *Generalization* — The main idea is presented along with subtopics that support the main idea. Students should look for the main idea at different places in the paragraph.

- *Problem solving* — This pattern can take different forms: (a) a solution following in the form of hypothetical solutions, (b) no solution, (c) a solution, (d) a question and a solution. Students should learn to identify the problem before finding the solution.

- *Comparison or contrast* — Ideas are presented through comparison and contrast. Although these two patterns are closely related, students usually do not have a problem differentiating between them. Readers can refer back to information given in preceding paragraphs to better understand the contrast or comparison.

- *Sequence* — A process or experiment is explained in steps. Students usually need to be encouraged to read slowly, striving to understand each step in turn.

MATHEMATICS

Math books are often written by mathematicians unaware of the reading levels of students who will use the book. Too often much of the written material is beyond the reach of many students. For example, a seventh grade math text may be written at a tenth grade level, making it out of reach for the on grade level reader.

Math texts present other problems as well. More than one symbol system is being used, since the language of mathematics consists of math numerals, words, signs, and letters. In addition, math texts do not provide the contextual clues present in traditional expository writing.

Students who can read mathematics textbooks with some success display the following skills: they know math symbols and vocabulary, they are precise in reading, they can follow directions and understand visuals, they are able to visualize, and they read analytically.

Mathematics vocabulary presents a real challenge because of the technical words unique to mathematics and because many general words such as *power, root,* and *product* take on different meanings in math. It is the responsibility of mathematics teachers to teach these special words since their meanings are unique to that subject. Through observation and informal vocabulary inventories teachers can determine which students need extra help with vocabulary. Teachers need to help pupils develop a background of experience, and guided reading activities can be especially appropriate. Study techniques such as SQ3R can also be used.

Math probably requires more rereading than any other subject. Students must read slowly, intensively, and precisely because of the special symbols and unique syntax. Of course, materials dealing with the history or the future of mathematics are usually written in an expository style and can therefore be read at a faster rate.

Robinson[18] has identified three patterns of writing in mathematics: concept development, principle development, and problem solution.

- *Concept development* — Presents operational mathematical concepts needed to solve problems. Students must learn to observe all elements in the passage and reread when necessary.
- *Principle development* — Presents a series of mathematical concepts from which students develop generalizations.

They must develop the generalization before they can solve the problems. As with concept development, the student must read carefully, observe all elements, and reread when necessary.

- *Problem solution* — Presents problem exercises for students to solve. Thomas and Robinson (*Improving Reading in Every Class*, pp. 316-317) detail seven steps that help students read problem-solving writing patterns:

> Step 1 — Read the problem thoroughly, asking, "What is this all about?"
>
> Step 2 — Reread the problem asking, "What am I to find here?"
>
> Step 3 — Ask yourself, "What facts are given?"
>
> Step 4 — Next, "What is my plan of attack?"
>
> Step 5 — Estimate the answer.
>
> Step 6 — Carry out the operations.
>
> Step 7 — Check your work.

Reading is a part of a mathematics program. Teachers can be more successful in teaching mathematics if they devote some energy and class time to improving students' reading skills in this content area.

SOCIAL STUDIES

The content and teaching of social studies have changed greatly in the past twenty years. The inquiry mode of teaching requires students to read widely, and many other materials are being used in addition to textbooks. Teachers expect students to think analytically and critically, and students are taught to identify propaganda and other forms of bias, separate fact from fiction, define and analyze issues, and read maps, charts, tables, and so forth. In addition, the writing style of middle school social studies materials is almost completely expository, and it is often difficult to isolate the main idea from the supporting details.

There is an increase in the use of primary sources; that is, the material is reprinted as it appeared originally, in the form of newspaper articles, documents, and so on. Certainly, this is a recommended practice, but it exposes students to materials very different from the usual textbook fare. Even mature readers occasionally have difficulty understanding phrases in primary sources.

Vocabulary in social studies is not one large body of technical words as is the case in science and mathematics. Each area of study within social studies has its own special vocabulary. It is usually not possible to teach every unfamiliar word, so teachers need to select those words students need for concept and generalization development. Before each chapter or unit, the teacher can use a simple word-matching activity to indicate which words students need to learn.

Guided reading activities are useful for teachers of social studies. When using this approach, background information can be supplied through films, slides, tapes, guest speakers, field trips, lectures, and discussions. The SQ3R study method is also helpful to students reading social studies materials.

Robinson[17] lists seven major patterns of writing common to social studies materials: topic development, enumeration, generalization, sequence, comparison or contrast, cause-effect, and question-answer.

- *Topic development* — This pattern presents all main ideas related to a topic. Students sometimes have difficulty differentiating between the topic of a passage and the main idea of a paragraph. Sometimes the topic is listed in the heading and is not directly referred to in the passage even though all main ideas are about the topic. Teachers need to help students realize that these main ideas are related to a topic.

- *Enumeration* — A series of subtopics in a paragraph are presented. An outline of subtopics under the main topic will help students see how these ideas are interrelated.

- *Generalization* — This pattern presents the generalization before or after the supporting information. Some students can find the generalization by simply reading a few paragraphs; others may need to outline.

- *Sequence* — In this pattern information is given in sequential steps. Readers cannot miss a step or they may not comprehend the entire passage. Some readers find it difficult to separate unimportant information from the sequential steps, and sometimes it can be helpful to skim a passage before reading, in order to identify the sequential steps.

- *Comparison or contrast* — This common pattern presents information through comparison and contrast, either within individual paragraphs or entire passages. It is often useful to ask students to list the differences and similarities of things being compared.
- *Cause-effect* — This pattern presents happenings or effects and their causes. Students should be taught to first skim the material, listing effects and locating their causes.
- *Question-answer* — This pattern consists of a question followed by several paragraphs or pages to answer it. Students can be helped to deal effectively with this style by asking them to focus on the question and then locate the answer(s).

ENGLISH

Literature in the middle school ranges from selections of poetry to essays to articles from newspapers and magazines. All students in a class should not be asked to read the same selections since reading abilities and interests vary widely. Literature assignments need to be made taking into account individual reading levels, backgrounds, and interests.

The reading of literature requires particular skills, including: analyzing characters, recognizing the climax, following a plot, reading dialect, and reading plays. Each literary style is different and requires that students utilize different reading abilities. For example, in poetry students are called upon to infer meaning from brief or obscure phrases.

Literature, unlike other content areas, has little vocabulary that is unique to it, except those words that describe writing style. The vocabulary to be presented depends on the particular selection and the vocabulary of the students.

The reading rate varies with each type of selection. Poetry is generally read more slowly than prose; however, the reader's familiarity with the material also influences the rate.

As in the other content areas, teachers must guide readers and pay particular attention to the first step of guided reading — building an experience range. Guided reading activities help ensure that readers will understand what they read.

CONCLUSION

Content area teachers need to be able to teach students those reading skills related to their content areas and make provisions to accommodate readers at all levels of ability. All middle school teachers face an enormous task — they need to provide learning environments that facilitate the growth of students' understanding in all areas of the curriculum. Teachers who are able to teach reading in their content areas are better equipped to meet this formidable challenge.

CHAPTER 6
READING IN RELATED
AREAS OF THE CURRICULUM

The ability to read is a vital measure of student success in most areas of the middle school curriculum. Some areas, however, require only minimum amounts of reading, and in these areas students can succeed without being unduly handicapped by reading deficiencies. Nonreaders may receive high grades in an area like physical education because of psychomotor abilities.

Some educators incorrectly assume that textbooks for non-academic areas are written at lower reading levels than those for academic subjects. On the contrary, these texts are usually written on grade level or even two or three years above grade level.

NONACADEMIC AREAS OF THE CURRICULUM

Several so-called nonacademic subjects are offered in many middle schools: home arts, health, physical education, art, music, and industrial arts.

MUSIC

Although the study of music does not emphasize traditional reading skills, music does require the decoding and comprehending of more than one symbol system: notes; symbols for rhythm, volume, and tempo; and the lyrics. In addition, music has its own technical vocabulary. Pronunciation presents a challenge to students and teachers since many words are of Italian origin. Basic word recognition skills are important in sight reading, but repeated rehearsals minimize this problem since students can usually memorize words as they practice.

Musical theory presents reading problems for even the best students. Guided reading activities are helpful here. Fortunately, only a small number of students read music theory at the middle school level.

When students are called on to read about the history of music and the lives of composers, a different type of comprehension is required. The study of music history usually involves discussion of cause and effect relationships and categorization. Music teachers should guide reading assignments in this area.

Reading rate varies. Material on music theory usually requires very slow reading with much rereading. Biographies of composers can generally be read much more rapidly. Students should be encouraged to practice silent reading of musical notation and lyrics before singing or playing. This increases accuracy and speed.

Music teachers can supplement music lessons with films and records that build background information. Public libraries offer a wide variety of books on music for teachers and students.

ART

At first thought, one would suppose that art does not require much reading. However, good readers have an advantage here, as in other subjects. Most art books are written for mature readers, and art textbooks are often written two or three years above the grade level for which they are intended. Written directions for complex art processes require careful reading.

Each area of art — sculpture, ceramics, and painting — has its own highly specialized vocabulary. Special terms must be introduced and explained.

Guided reading activities can be valuable here, and teachers should consider borrowing films and slides from public libraries and museums to build background for students.

HOME ARTS

Teachers unfamiliar with the current curriculum of home economics, or home arts as it is usually called in the middle school, are in for a surprise. In addition to cooking and sewing, students of both sexes study child growth and development, parenting, housing patterns, consumer education, home management, and much more. Reading skills are important for understanding the course content. Although a textbook may be used, it usually represents only a small portion of the printed material available. Government pamphlets, consumer education magazines, and home care information can be used by students as lifelong references.

Home arts textbooks are not easy to read; they are usually technical and factual and do not provide glossaries or other aids for understanding specialized terms. A number of different kinds of reading patterns are presented: (1) giving directions for doing things around the home; (2) providing information on such topics as child growth and development; and (3) presenting diagrams for operating home appliances. Home arts teachers can help students by offering guided reading assignments. Since students are familiar with home living in some form, it is relatively easy for teachers to build background experiences. In most cases, items that can be used to explain vocabulary are on hand in the classroom. Study techniques such as the SQ3R method (see Chapter 5) are recommended.

Reading proficiency in home arts brings both immediate and long term rewards. If students follow the recipe, the cake will be a success. If they read and absorb the information and techniques that fall under the province of home arts, they will refer to this body of knowledge over and over again in the years to come.

INDUSTRIAL ARTS

The courses in industrial arts are concerned with helping students learn to participate effectively in an industrial/technological society. Reading is important here if students are to get the most out of the course. It is vital for those students who need to read instructions and learn new material as they engage in leisure time activities such as woodworking, or choose careers in industrial arts.

Textbooks in industrial arts are usually written two or more steps above grade level and require students to do quite a bit of abstract thinking as well as sift through innumerable facts. The student is expected to: (1) understand specialized vocabulary; (2) comprehend factual information; (3) follow directions on the use of tools and equipment; (4) interpret information from technical materials; and (5) interpret diagrams and other types of graphics.

In teaching vocabulary, teachers should make frequent references to real items and experiences via field trips, patterns, models, and films. Because course content is so accessible, teachers have an ideal setting in which to explain vocabulary and provide the background information necessary for meaningful reading.

Three patterns of writing are found in industrial arts materials: (1) information format to explain a process; (2) directions format to explain how to do something; and (3) directions format with diagrams or other visuals to explain how to do something. Reading rates are usually slow, especially when the material includes diagrams. Students should be encouraged to read and reread the material until they understand it. Guided reading activities can be helpful in this content area.

PHYSICAL EDUCATION

Most middle school students greatly admire their physical education teachers. These teachers can take advantage of their exalted position to help students become better readers by encouraging them to improve study habits and put forth additional effort in the academic areas.

Reading content in physical education is one of three types: (1) rules for playing games; (2) techniques for improvement in sports and recreational activities; and (3) material about sports figures and great sports events. Reading skills required include: (1) understanding the technical words peculiar to each sport; (2) following directions; and (3) interpreting rules and illustrations.

Vocabulary skills are especially important in physical education, because without the appropriate vocabulary students cannot interpret rules or understand directions about techniques. Physical education teachers should encourage students to increase their understanding and enjoyment of physical education by doing recreational reading in this area.

HEALTH

Whether health instruction is a separate subject area or combined with physical education or home arts, there are printed materials designed to be read by middle school students. Both health and first aid materials are "fact packed." They are usually written in expository form, two or more grade levels higher than the instructional reading level of the students. Due to the variety of subjects discussed, the readability can vary greatly within a single book. If you are using a readability formula with health materials, be sure to take several samples from different parts of the book.

Guided reading activities (see Chapter 5) are recommended in this area. Health teachers usually do not have problems building background information because they can make reference to the students' own experiences. Although the vocabulary is technical, most words are of a practical nature and students often use them in daily conversation and writing.

CHAPTER 7
JUST FOR THE FUN OF IT —
RECREATIONAL READING

A major objective of middle school education should be the promotion of recreational reading. This responsibility falls not only to language arts teachers and media specialists. It is every teacher's responsibility to model reading behavior, allow time for students to read, display books, and reward students for reading. Even physical education teachers can be instrumental by letting students see them carrying or reading books and encouraging students to discuss books they are reading, especially in the area of sports.

There is a great deal of competition for students' out-of-school hours. Television is a prime contender, along with community clubs, church, and sports. Students who come from nonreading families find it particularly difficult to make time for recreational reading. Parents who value reading set aside time for reading and make trips to the library part of the family's regular activities.

VALUES OF RECREATIONAL READING

There are many benefits to be derived from recreational reading: an increase in vocabulary, an improved attitude toward reading, the refinement of reading skills, and the realization that leisure time reading can provide pleasure, impart information, and broaden one's range of experience.

INCREASE IN VOCABULARY

Students who read for recreation come in contact with a wide variety of reading materials written at different levels of difficulty. As they read they meet words time and time again in different contexts. In fact, recreational reading is one of the best ways to build vocabulary.

IMPROVED ATTITUDE TOWARD READING

Remedial readers are not the only students with poor attitudes toward reading; some better readers read only when required. Some reading programs teach students to read but do not help them develop a love of reading.

Attitudes toward reading improve when middle school teachers read good literature to their students, enthusiastically sharing the special magic a skilled author can weave. Students need to hear the beauty of language, and time should be set aside on a regular basis for this important activity.

Teachers can also help middle schoolers find books written at their interest and ability levels. Remedial readers are "turned off" when asked to read stories clearly intended for younger children. Help change their negative attitudes by suggesting recreational reading in high-interest, low-vocabulary books. Many bibliographies are available for this purpose.

REFINEMENT OF READING SKILLS

Some educators mistakenly believe that reading skills can only be learned in direct skills lessons. Direct skills instruction may be necessary for some students, but not the best approach for others. Recreational reading is absolutely essential to the development and improvement of reading attitudes and abilities.

LEISURE TIME READING CAN PROVIDE PLEASURE

Regretfully too many students and adults do not read in their leisure time. Prophets of doom say that reading is an obsolete skill, that the computer and other forms of communication make reading a slow way to process information. Even if reading is "inefficient," it will continue to be a pleasant leisure time activity.

HOW TO ENCOURAGE RECREATIONAL READING

Recreational reading is a valuable activity for the middle schooler. Teachers can encourage recreational reading in many ways: (1) give them what they want; (2) model reading behaviors;

(3) make books readily available; (4) provide time to read; (5) encourage sharing.

GIVE THEM WHAT THEY WANT

Some middle school students report they do not like the materials they are asked to read. Some teachers demand that students read only "good" literature, that is, the classics. We are not opposed to good literature, but experienced teachers know that these selections do not always accommodate readers' interests. Students should be given the freedom to select the books they read for pleasure. Teachers can do their part by providing books that meet the varying interests of their students.

An interest inventory can help teachers pinpoint students' interests and will provide information about students' overall reading habits. The following inventory can be modified to meet individual needs.

INTEREST INVENTORY

1. My favorite magazine is ——————————.
2. My favorite book is ——————————.
3. The part of the newspaper I read first is ——————.
4. If I could be anywhere in the world,
   I would like to be in ——————————.
5. The best vehicle on wheels is ——————————.
6. My favorite musical group is ——————————.
7. My favorite pop song is ——————————.
8. My favorite television program is ——————————.
9. The food I like best is ——————————.
10. My favorite thing to do on
    Saturday afternoon is ——————————.
11. My mother likes to read ——————————.
12. My father likes to read ——————————.
13. I like to get exercise by ——————————.
14. My favorite person in history was ——————————.

MODEL READING BEHAVIORS

Students will gain a new appreciation for reading if they see teachers carrying, reading, and discussing books. Students who have nonreading parents or are influenced by other nonreading adults especially need contact with adult models who like to read.

MAKE BOOKS READILY AVAILABLE

"Books everywhere" should be the motto of middle schools. Book displays need not be exceptionally elaborate. Middle schoolers often approach a table heaped with paperbacks more eagerly than a book display that has been beautifully decorated and arranged. Fader's *The New Hooked on Books*[8] is filled with suggestions for getting students to read simply by making books readily available.

PROVIDE TIME TO READ

Hopefully, teachers and administrators in the middle school agree that recreational reading during the school day is a productive use of time. It may be difficult to evaluate the direct effects of recreational reading, but it is still one of the best ways to aid learning and improve attitudes toward reading.

No matter how crowded the curriculum, there has to be some time alloted to recreational reading. One way to do this is through SSR or Sustained Silent Reading. SSR is a period during the school day when everyone, including the teacher, reads silently for pleasure. SSR ensures that all students have some time during the day to read for pleasure. In addition, SSR gives middle schoolers a chance to see the teacher reading for pleasure.

ENCOURAGE BOOK SHARING

The old-fashioned practice of writing book reports may discourage more reading than it encourages. It is not hard to see that if students have to write extensive reports on every book they read, they will not be eager to read many books. Books can be shared in several more appealing ways, some of which are described below.

SHARING THROUGH FORMS

As a substitute for traditional book reports, the teacher can ask students to complete forms such as these:

FORM 1

Student's name _____

Title of book _____

Author _____

It took me _____ hours to read the book.

The most exciting part was on page _____.

My favorite character was _____.

Everybody should read this book: Yes   No

Choose one:

I like the way the book ended because _____.

I did not like the way the book ended because _____.

My favorite incident was _____.

My least favorite incident was _____.

FORM 2

(for reluctant readers)

Student's name _____

Title of book _____

Author _____

The story took place in _____.

The main character was _____.

The way the story ended was _____.

The type of person who should
    read this book is _____.

FORM 3

(for remedial readers)

Student's name _____

Title of book _____

Author _____

Choose one:
I liked this book because _____ .
I did not like this book because _____ .

Choose one:
Other students should read this book because _____
_____ .

Other students should not read this book because _____
_____ .

OTHER WAYS OF SHARING

Book sharing works best when teachers make available many activities or ways to share books and allow students to select the activity that appeals most to them.

1. *Creative dramatics with books* — Students who enjoy creative dramatics can choose to dramatize one or more parts of a book they have read. Give students a chance to prepare and practice their story before performing it in front of the class. Costuming may or may not be used.

2. *Construction type activities* — Many students enjoy constructing dioramas or scale models. Construction materials can be furnished by the school or by the student. If possible, allow time during the day when students can work on their constructions. Windowsills, bookcases, walls, and ceilings can all be used for display purposes.

3. *Book characters* — Some students enjoy making book characters for display in the room. Puppets are popular, especially bowling pin figures, papier-mâché figures, sock puppets, and paper bag puppets.

4. *Booklets* — Middle schoolers enjoy making booklets or

scrapbooks featuring scenes from a book or samples of creative writing inspired by a favorite book or author.

5. *Book posters* — Posters can be completed in a short time and require little in the way of materials. "Wanted" posters featuring book characters are often of interest to middle school students.

6. *Other projects* — Make book jackets; advertise books; make book trees; group students according to interests to facilitate sharing books on the same interest level; organize a book club.

IN CONCLUSION

Many activities, including academics, compete for the attention of teachers and middle school students. Once students are motivated to do recreational reading, it is up to teachers to provide time, space, and materials. Although recreational reading is generally one of the most neglected areas in the middle school curriculum, it must be given higher priority if students are to develop into better, more enthusiastic readers.

CHAPTER 8
EVALUATION OF THE
READING PROGRAM

How do you determine if you have a quality reading program in your classroom or in the total middle school? Many educators judge their own reading program by administering a standardized reading test and comparing their school's scores with scores from schools across the nation. We believe that standardized reading tests have very little, if any, value. There are other more important considerations to keep in mind when evaluating a reading program:

1. The attitudes of the students toward reading
2. The number of students who are making expected progress in reading
3. The amount of printed material read by the students
4. The number of students reading content area materials at instructional and independent levels, as well as the number working at frustration levels
5. The amount of time spent instructing individual students in reading compared to the amount spent in group activities
6. The teachers' attitudes toward reading
7. The overall responsiveness of the school to the reading needs of middle school students.

A discussion of each aspect follows.

THE ATTITUDES OF STUDENTS TOWARD READING

Students' attitudes are best measured intuitively, and it doesn't take very long to sense negative or positive attitudes toward reading. Usually teachers are quick to report students' general attitude toward reading in their school.

The following questionnaire is a sample of the type that can be used to assess attitudes toward reading. Teachers may modify the individual items to fit their own purposes. Although some of the items refer to learning preferences, most reveal students' attitudes toward reading. For remedial students, try using these items in an interview format.

FEELINGS ABOUT READING

1. I like to read best when _____ .
2. The worst part of reading is _____ .
3. I could learn to read better if _____ .
4. The thing that bugs me most
   about reading is _____ .
5. Reading becomes a drag when _____ .
6. The easiest thing about reading is _____ .
7. The best thing the teacher does
   to help me read is _____ .
8. The words I can't pronounce are usually _____ .
9. The hardest part of reading is _____ .
10. Reading is necessary because _____ .

THE NUMBER OF STUDENTS MAKING EXPECTED PROGRESS IN READING

We think that it is difficult, if not impossible, to measure students' reading potentials. It is, however, possible to determine if students are making progress in reading. We do not advocate the use of formulas to determine expectancy levels or the use of devices such as scattergrams. A student of average intelligence who has no serious learning disabilities should be making reading progress close to grade level. But a middle school student of superior intelligence should be making rapid progress toward becoming a mature reader.

Schools whose students show high achievement scores sometimes assume that they have a quality reading program and that all students are making progress in reading. This may or may not be the case; there is a high correlation between the socioeconomic level of students in a school and the reading scores in that school. Schools in high socioeconomic areas probably will rank high even if the reading program is not superior. Schools in very low socioeconomic areas may have an excellent reading program, yet show low reading scores. High achievement scores may make excellent public relations, but they should not be the single means of evaluating the reading program in a middle school.

In recent years, criterion-referenced tests have received some attention. A criterion-referenced test measures specific skills and shows whether or not a student has mastered these skills. Such test scores can be helpful in evaluating a reading program, particularly when planning instruction for individual students. Again, however, these test scores should not be the single means of judging the reading program.

Of course, teacher observation is one way to determine if a student is making progress. Teachers can note: (1) at what level of difficulty the student is reading; (2) the number of times a student asks for assistance with words; (3) the growth of the student's vocabulary; (4) the number of minutes a student reads each day; (5) the amount of material the student takes home to read; and (6) the confidence a student shows in reading and that student's willingness to assist classmates.

What about students' self-evaluations? Students who feel they are making progress will continue to make progress. The following questionnaire can help students document their progress. Teachers can modify the questionnaire to meet their own needs.

READING PROGRESS SELF-REPORT

1. (Circle one.) I feel my reading *has improved — has not improved.*

2. In the last two months I have learned the following new words:

   _____

3. In the last two months I have read the following books or stories in addition to my regular textbook assignments:

   _____

4. I know that my reading is *improving* or *not improving* because

   _____
   _____ .

THE AMOUNT OF PRINTED MATERIAL READ BY STUDENTS

Teachers cannot accurately predict if middle school students will read as adults, but they can assess current reading patterns. Of course, this does not mean that teachers should count the number of pages students read. A better measure can be had by looking at the student's content area and recreational reading.

Do students read their textbook assignments and materials related to content area learning activities? Some students carry textbooks to and from class, open their books during class discussions, yet never really read a sentence. In some classrooms, it is possible to participate in discussions, answer questions, and even take a test without ever having read the assignment.

Do students read for recreation? Some schools count the number of students who check out books and the number of books borrowed to get some idea of students' recreational reading habits. As with other types of reading measurement, caution must be exercised since some students check out material that they do not read.

THE NUMBER OF STUDENTS READING CONTENT AREA MATERIALS AT INSTRUCTIONAL AND INDEPENDENT LEVELS

In some schools a large percentage of the students are reading at frustration levels. Teachers report that in middle schools where they teach, few materials are geared to the instructional levels of their students. This is often the case when books are purchased for the entire school system instead of giving due consideration to the individual school's needs or to the needs of a particular class.

Chapter 3 covered ways to determine if pupils are reading at independent, instructional, or frustration level. The cloze technique, discussed in Chapter 5, is a good way to determine if students can comprehend the textbook or other printed material.

THE AMOUNT OF TIME SPENT INSTRUCTING INDIVIDUAL STUDENTS

All middle school students may not need an individualized,

one-to-one reading approach, but if students who are having reading difficulties are going to improve, they should receive some individual attention. In a middle school of 900 students, there may be only 50 students in need of extra time and attention. Whether or not they receive this help is one indicator of the quality of that school's reading program.

TEACHERS' ATTITUDES TOWARD READING

If teachers were asked, most would probably say they possess favorable attitudes toward reading. However, are these attitudes observable? Do teachers act as appropriate models for their students? Do teachers read during their spare time at home and at school? Do students see teachers enjoying reading? Do middle schoolers know which teachers like to read? Do they know what books teachers are reading?

THE RESPONSIVENESS OF THE SCHOOL TO THE READING NEEDS OF THE STUDENTS

Think about the following questions to determine if your school is responsive to the reading needs of students.

Is staffing adequate for a quality reading program? Some middle schools totally ignore reading. In other schools there may not be enough teachers to cover all needs. In this case content area teachers can compensate for the lack of specialized staff.

Are appropriate materials being provided for the reading program? If the total school views reading as important, money will be allocated to purchase whatever is needed.

What about scheduling? Time for reading instruction must be planned. Reading needs must be accommodated even if other curriculum areas suffer. If no time is allotted or if the time is very short, little or no reading instruction will occur.

In some schools staff and scheduling are adequate, but large class size prohibits teachers from being effective. In order to ensure that remedial readers make progress, individual attention is necessary. This is virtually impossible in large classes.

Are content area teachers really taking every opportunity to teach reading? It is not enough to hire a reading specialist and provide all the elements necessary to a good developmental and remedial reading program. Content area teachers must incorporate reading instruction into regular lessons. As explained in Chapter 5, we are not suggesting a full remedial program in the individual classrooms, but rather reading instruction appropriate for each content area.

How often should the reading program be evaluated? A certain amount of evaluation should be part of a teacher's daily routine. Periodic evaluation should take place at least once a year to determine program strengths and weaknesses. Evaluation of the reading program is the ongoing responsibility of the total school staff and not just the job of individuals from the central office.

NOTES

NOTES

[1] Allen, Roach Van. *Language Experiences in Communication.* Boston: Houghton Mifflin Co., 1976.

[2] Barbe, Walter B., and Abbott, Jerry L. *Personalized Reading Instruction: New Techniques that Increase Reading Skill and Comprehension.* West Nyack, New York: Parker Publishing Co., 1975.

[3] Bormuth, John. "The Cloze Readability Procedure." *Elementary English* 45:429-436; April 1968.

[4] Burmeister, Lou E. *Reading Strategies for Middle and Secondary School Teachers.* Reading, Massachusetts: Addison-Wesley Publishing Co., 1978, p. 342.

[5] _____. *Words — From Print to Meaning.* Reading, Massachusetts: Addison-Wesley Publishing Co., 1975.

[6] Coopersmith, Stanley. *The Antecedents of Self-Esteem.* San Francisco: W. H. Freeman, 1967.

[7] Dolch, E. W. *The Basic Sight Word Test.* Champaign, Illinois: Garrard Publishing Co., 1942.

[8] Fader, Daniel, and others. *The New Hooked on Books.* New York: Berkley Publishing Corp., 1976.

[9] Fillmer, H. Thompson. "The Middle Schoolers' Reading Program." *Language Arts* 52: 1123-1126; November-December 1975.

[10] Fry, Edward. *Reading Instruction for Classroom and Clinic.* New York: McGraw-Hill, 1972.

[11] _____. *The Emergency Reading Teacher's Manual.* Highland Park, New Jersey: Dreier Educational Systems, 1974, p. 16.

[12] Goodlad, John I. *School, Curriculum, and the Individual.* Waltham, Massachusetts: Blaisdell, 1966, p. 34.

[13] Goodman, Kenneth S. *Miscue Analysis: Applications to Reading Instruction.* Urbana, Illinois: National Council of Teachers of English, 1973.

[14] Potter, Thomas C., and Rae, Gwermeth. *Informal Reading Diagnosis: A Practical Guide for the Classroom Teacher.* Englewood Cliffs, New Jersey: Prentice-Hall, 1973.

[15] Robinson, Francis P. *Effective Study.* New York: Harper and Row, 1961.

[16] Robinson, H. Alan. *Teaching Reading and Study Strategies: The Content Areas.* Boston: Allyn and Bacon, 1975, pp. 100-124.

[17] *Ibid.*, pp. 135-136.

[18] *Ibid.*, pp. 169-186.

[19] Sanders, Norris M. *Classroom Questions: What Kinds?* New York: Harper and Row, 1966.

[20] Sivarolli, Nicholas J. *Classroom Reading Inventory.* Dubuque, Iowa: William C. Brown., 1973.

[21] Spache, Evelyn B. *Reading Activities for Child Involvement.* Boston: Allyn and Bacon, 1976.

[22] Strickland, Joann H., and Alexander, William. "Seeking Continuity in Early and Middle School Education" in *Education for the Middle School Years: Readings.* (Edited by James E. Hertling and Howard G. Getz.) Glenview, Illinois: Scott, Foresman and Co., 1971, pp. 9-14; p. 11.

ANNOTATED BIBLIOGRAPHY

ANNOTATED BIBLIOGRAPHY

Adler, Mortimer J., and Van Doren, Charles. *How to Read a Book.* New
York: Simon and Schuster, 1972.
Discusses the levels of reading and how students respond to those
levels. Also gives ways to approach different types of reading and lists
goals of reading. The book is a rewritten version of a 1940s bestseller.

Aukerman, Robert C. *Reading in the Secondary School Classroom.* New York:
McGraw-Hill Book Co., 1972.
Contains chapters that relate to all academic subjects in the secondary
school. Very comprehensive in the treatment of general issues in
reading instruction and in guidelines for each content area.

Aulls, Mark W. *Developmental and Remedial Reading in the Middle Grades.*
Boston: Allyn and Bacon, 1978.
Describes ways to implement developmental and remedial reading
instruction in middle grade classrooms. The areas discussed include
comprehension, reading rate, writing and reading relationships,
diagnosis, decoding, individualizing, and resources.

Burmeister, Lou E. *Reading Strategies for Middle and Secondary School Teachers.*
Reading, Massachusetts: Addison-Wesley Publishing Co., 1978.
Provides ideas for content area teachers. The author suggests: (1)
ways to adjust reading materials for students, (2) strategies for teaching
reading in content areas, and (3) how to use school resources in the
reading program as the entire staff works cooperatively.

Clark, Leonard H. *Teaching Social Studies in Secondary Schools.* New York:
Macmillan Publishing Co., 1973.
Contains a chapter on reading and study related specifically to the
teaching of social studies. Excellent, practical suggestions for reading
critically. The section on selecting and using textbooks will assist social
studies teachers.

Dillner, Martha H., and Olson, Joanne P. *Personalizing Reading Instruction in
Middle, Junior, and Senior High Schools.* New York: Macmillan
Publishing Co., 1977.

Contains five major parts: (1) the meaning of reading, (2) reading needs and classroom materials, (3) diagnostic/prescriptive teaching, (4) effective reading programs, and (5) teaching reading. The book utilizes a competency-based instructional system.

Duffy, Gerald G., editor. *Reading in the Middle School*. Newark, Delaware: International Reading Association, 1975.
Contains twenty chapters written by several different authorities. The book describes middle schools and discusses appropriate reading instruction for middle school students now and in the future.

Earle, Richard A. *Teaching Reading and Mathematics*. Newark, Delaware: International Reading Association, 1976.
Includes a thorough discussion of both the mathematics process and reading process. Detailed suggestions are given for teaching each writing pattern that exists in mathematics content material. The appendices are invaluable to mathematics teachers because they contain lists of words that appear most frequently in mathematics texts, lists of high-interest materials for mathematics classrooms, and other practical materials.

Estes, Thomas H., and Vaughan, Joseph L., Jr. *Reading and Learning in the Content Classroom*. Boston: Allyn and Bacon, 1978.
Describes diagnostic and instructional techniques in content area instruction.

Fry, Edward. *The Emergency Reading Teacher's Manual*. Highland Park, New Jersey: Dreier Educational Systems, 1974.
Provides a brief overview of reading instruction. Contents include: (1) assessment of reading abilities, (2) selection of appropriate materials, (3) comprehension, (4) phonics, and (5) instant words.

Hafner, Lawrence, E. *Developmental Reading in Middle and Secondary Schools: Foundations, Strategies, and Skills for Teaching*. New York: Macmillan Publishing Co., 1977.
Presents basic ideas about reading instruction and gives strategies for teaching vocabulary, comprehension, and study skills. One section focuses on the teaching of reading in specific content areas. The book is directed toward teachers who wish to improve the reading skills of average and superior readers.

Hafner, Lawrence E., editor. *Improving Reading in Middle and Secondary Schools.* New York: Macmillan Publishing Co., 1974.
Presents a large number of articles on various facets of teaching reading at the middle and secondary school levels. Areas covered include: word recognition, comprehension, research, reading rate, and reading in the content areas.

Laffey, James L., editor. *Reading in the Content Areas.* Newark, Delaware: International Reading Association, 1972.
Describes recent research findings on content reading (literature, mathematics, science, and social studies) and discusses implications of this research to classroom instruction.

McIntyre, Virgie M. *Reading Strategies and Enrichment Activities for Grades 4-9.* Columbus: Charles E. Merrill Publishing Co., 1977.
Discusses specific strategies for teaching reading improvement in the areas of vocabulary, study skills, motivation and interest, comprehension, and rate. Also included are ideas for diagnosing students' word attack and comprehension abilities.

Miller, Wilma H. *Reading Correction Kit.* West Nyack, New York: The Center for Applied Research in Education, Inc., 1975.
Provides ideas for developing corrective or remedial reading instruction in the areas of sight words, phonics, structional analysis, context, dictionary and glossary, vocabulary, comprehension, and study skills. The author describes the skills, describes how to use the corrective devices to teach those skills, and provides actual samples of the corrective devices including worksheets, exercises, and games.

Miller, Wilma H. *Reading Diagnosis Kit.* New York: The Center for Applied Research in Education, Inc., 1974.
Includes major standardized and informal diagnostic devices for assessing reading difficulties, and offers tips for making accurate diagnoses.

Miller, Wilma H. *Teaching Reading in the Secondary School.* Springfield, Illinois: Charles C. Thomas, 1974.
Directed at the content area teacher, this book details several aspects of secondary school reading, including word recognition, comprehension, rate and diagnostic tests.

Piercey, Dorothy. *Reading Activities in Content Areas.* Boston: Allyn and Bacon, 1976.
Part One of the book focuses on teacher techniques. Part Two focuses on activities for students in most of the subject areas.

Reiter, Irene M. *Why Can't They Read It?* Philadelphia: Polaski Co., 1974.
Presents actual excerpts from content area material with a discussion of the readability factors found in each sample. Teaching suggestions make this a very practical content area reading source. George Spache was the reading consultant for this book.

Robinson, H. Alan. *Teaching Reading and Study Strategies: The Content Areas.* Boston: Allyn and Bacon, 1975.
Contains ideas on reading the different patterns of writing common to various content areas. Gives teaching and learning strategies common to all content areas and strategies unique to each subject area.

Robinson, H. Alan, and Thomas, Ellen Lamar. *Fusing Reading Skills and Content.* Newark, Delaware: International Reading Association, 1969.
Contains a collection of papers presented at the 1969 International Reading Association Convention meeting on "Reading in the Secondary School Curriculum." Numerous content areas are discussed in this practical volume written for classroom teachers.

Shepherd, David L. *Comprehensive High School Reading Methods.* Columbus, Ohio: Charles E. Merrill Publishing Co., 1973.
Examines each content area's reading materials with specific suggestions for teaching reading at the secondary level. The introductory chapters explore the reading process, drawing implications for the secondary reading curriculum.

Shuman, R. Baird. *Strategies in Teaching Reading: Secondary.* Washington, D.C.: National Education Association, 1978.
Provides reading instruction ideas for middle and secondary school teachers. The areas described include the nonreader, oral reading, newspapers and the teaching of reading, and miscue analysis.

Spache, Evelyn B. *Reading Activities for Child Involvement.* Boston: Allyn and Bacon, 1976.
Presents 400 reading activities that are appropriate or can be adapted

for use with middle school students in need of specific skill development in reading.

Thomas, Ellen Lamar, and Robinson, H. Alan. *Improving Reading in Every Class*. Boston: Allyn and Bacon, 1972.
Suggests ways to teach basic processes in reading and ways to teach reading in most subject areas. The focus is on content area instruction, with specific suggestions given for developmental and corrective reading.

Wilson, Robert M. *Diagnostic and Remedial Reading for Classroom and Clinic*. Columbus: Charles E. Merrill Publishing Co., 1977.
Assumes that the reader has some experience with teaching reading and the foundations of reading. The book contains information on classroom and clinical diagnosis, and remediation activities for word attack and comprehension.